WOMEN LAWYERS AT WORK

Meet twelve prominent women lawyers who are practicing lawyers, judges, professors, and administrators. They work in the fields of tax law, labor law, trial law, copyright law, family law, and in various government positions. You'll get a view of the practical dimensions of daily life in the legal work places of America, as well as a look at their personal lives. These successful women come from a variety of family backgrounds and from all parts of the United States. You'll meet their families and see what it is like to have a mother who is a lawyer. You'll share both the rewards and hardships these women have experienced. Their stories show hard-working, determined individuals who overcame many obstacles to climb to the top of their profession.

Women Lawyers at Work

Elinor Porter Swiger

JULIAN MESSNER

NEW YORK

Manufactured in the United States of America

Design by Miriam Temple

Library of Congress Cataloging in Publication Data
Swiger, Elinor Porter.
Women lawyers at work.

Includes index.
SUMMARY: Examines the private and public aspects of the
lives of twelve prominent women lawyers.
1. Lawyers—United States—Biography—Juvenile literature.
2. Women lawyers—United States—Biography—Juvenile
literature.   [1. Women lawyers.   2. Lawyers]   I. Title.
KF372.S95   340′.092′2 [B] [920]   78–15270
ISBN 0–671–32909–X

CONTENTS

ACKNOWLEDGMENTS

I am, first and foremost, deeply grateful to each of the biographees for their generosity in supplying the facts and anecdotes which make each of the twelve biographies in this book a very special story. Their contributions helped to make each tale uniquely helpful to all readers and, most especially, to young women who expect to meet multiple responsibilities as mothers, wives, and successful lawyers. Knowing well the demands made on the busy biographees, I am most appreciative of their willingness to take time for the interviews and related chores. For the extras provided me—additional tapes, decades-old clippings, and more—special thanks.

Thanks are due also to the associates who kindly consented to interviews and supplied additional information and insights—secretaries, schedulers, and colleagues who work (or have worked) with biographees, and husbands and children who do (or did) share their off-duty hours.

I am grateful also for the invaluable assistance that I received from the talented staff at the Glenview Library and the affiliated Illinois State Library System.

In thinking of others "without whom this book could not have been written," a debt of a different order must be acknowledged. Grateful tribute is most surely due to those few far-sighted lawyers like Bob Mathews, former Professor of Law at The Ohio State University and elsewhere, who always believed that there was a place for women in the legal profession and encouraged them to study law at a time when most of the world did not.

INTRODUCTION

This book is about twelve women at the top. They are stars in the United States legal profession; all are talented and stunningly successful. For all their luster, the reader should know that I did not, and would not, presume to make a judgment that they represent *the* twelve foremost females in the American legal world. To attempt such a rating would be hazardous and, most surely, unfair to dozens of other distinguished women who are making impressive contributions to the profession every day.

It is also beyond the scope of this book to honor the women pioneers in the legal profession who played significant roles in easing the path of all of today's women lawyers. Only two decades ago in 1956, just two hundred and sixty women were graduated from all of the law schools in the United States. The total number of women who were members of the Bar was, until the past few years, painfully small. But their overall impact was substantial, and some individual women played stellar roles.

9

I have chosen, in this volume, to sketch the lives of twelve outstanding women attorneys from contemporary society who are performing representative kinds of legal work at the highest levels. Biographees are practicing lawyers, judges, professors, and administrators. Some are leaders in the Bar; several are authors and respected authorities in their particular fields of interest.

The women come from varied family backgrounds and from all parts of the United States. Their chosen life-styles range from unmarried to married with four children. Of widely varying ages, they were graduated from eight different law schools over a period of thirty years, from 1934 to 1964.

The biographees have, collectively and individually, compiled astonishing records of achievement. Tribute is due them—and it is a part of their stories. In each chapter, a larger portion of the text is devoted to detailing obstacles on the road to the top and, more importantly, the way in which these women cleared these hurdles.

During most of the years of their working lives, many doors of the legal profession were closed to them. The way in which the individual women thrust the "foot in" to force opens those doors forms the heart of each story. Their attitudes, and their personal experiences concerning sex discrimination, were varied. On the whole, the differences were less marked than the similarities of their encounters and views. Responses were uniformly creative.

Some of the women, like Carole Bellows, a state Bar Association President in Illinois, are people-oriented political personalities; others, like Elisabeth Owens of the Harvard Law School faculty, are library-oriented scholars. All are highly effective communicators.

The women who chose to combine careers with mother-hood faced special challenges. In the book, they share their views, their experiences, and their advice with the reader. All agree that, even in an enlightened age, the problems will not vanish. All agree that, with help, they are soluble.

Actress Katharine Hepburn, in a recent article in the *Ladies' Home Journal*, observed: "I'm not sure any woman can successfully pursue a career and be a good mother at the same time. The trouble with women today is that they want everything. But no one can have it all." The women about whom I write in this book have ample grounds on which to disagree. Mothers to a total of twenty-three children, and grandmothers to eight, they cherish family life. The young mothers testify that maternal obligations have top priority. The mature mothers, like mothers the world over, are proud of their successful adult children. They deny exerting pressure upon their offspring to choose legal careers. However, to date, six of the children are law graduates, one is in law school, and at least two of the younger children now say they will be lawyers.

In communities across the country, the women faced critical publics in past decades. Popular disdain for the working mother was widespread, molded by a near-unanimous media verdict that mother must be "in the home," to keep the kids "off the streets." When the children excelled, which was often, there was reassurance. When they faltered, or when illness or accident struck, confidence was tested. Judge Irene Scott, Louise Raggio, and Ruth Ginsburg each faced critical medical emergencies that kept them at a child's hospital bedside day and night during painful periods of extreme crisis.

Mostly, the busy mothers turned aside and strove to ignore or forget the remarks of their detractors and the well-meaning worriers. Many skipped P.T.A. meetings, but bent their schedules to make it to school plays and Little League games. Most went the extra mile to meet the added obligations of home, school, and community when children were young. Harriet Pilpel has written about her efforts and her frustrations in trying to fulfill all of her roles to perfection—at home and in the office.

Although the responses of the career-mothers to their special challenges varied, some common denominators in their success can be identified. In nearly every case, spouses were (and are) highly supportive, always in principle and, most often, in practice as well. With a few exceptions, they are men who are quick to lend a hand with household tasks and child care. Several are gourmet cooks; most are at home in the kitchen. They cheerfully take on other tasks. Judge Creighton Coleman has for years bought most of his wife Mary's clothing.

Biographees were uniformly described by colleagues as determined, hard-working individuals. Congresswoman Pat Schroeder got her first job at age fourteen; so did former National Labor Relations Board Chairman Betty Murphy.

All of the biographees excelled at early ages—in academic competition, in oratory, and, surprisingly often, in sports. Miami Law School Dean Soia Mentschikoff was captain of the basketball team at Hunter College; Carla Hills led the women's tennis squad at Stanford; Jewel LaFontant piloted the volleyball team during all of her undergraduate years at Oberlin College.

Without exception, the women describe themselves as "high energy" individuals. Some seldom get more than six hours sleep a night; many can run on less, at least for a time. There are two early birds; the others call themselves "night people." In spite of their preferences, they are, for the most part, up early every day in order to put in work weeks of sixty or seventy hours, or more.

Many, but not all, of the biographees knew from the time they were quite young that they wanted to be lawyers. It is significant, and somewhat startling in view of the tenor of the times, that only two of the women faced any opposition from parents concerning their plans to study law. Most reported that their parents were enthusiastic; that they had expected their daughters to pursue careers. In the case of most biographees, at least one parent was very strong, even pushy. Agnes Stallings badgered her shy teenaged daughter to interview Oliver Wendell Holmes. When the president of the University of Alabama discouraged daughter Irene in her plan to study law, father Arthur Feagin quickly dispatched a note of encouragement and, for inspiration, enclosed a clipping about a woman lawyer who had just been appointed to the U.S. Board of Tax Appeals. For the most part, they were parents who set high standards and steered their daughters toward constructive commitments early.

In undergraduate days, the women pursued a variety of courses, ranging from pre-med to Oriental Studies. Interestingly, not one of these successful lawyers said that she recommends a particular course of study to pre-law students. There was agreement on only one point: all pre-law students should perfect their writing skills, in the classroom and elsewhere.

The stories in this book are not standard biographies. I have not attempted to list all of the publications written by each biographee; nor all of the committees on which she has served. In most cases, the reader who seeks such information about individual biographees can find it in *Who's Who in American Women* and other sources. This volume is a specialized reference. This book is designed to provide for prospective law students and other interested readers glimpses into the personal and professional lives of some of America's most successful women—women who happen to be lawyers.

It is my hope that in reading their words and the accounts of their experiences the reader will be better informed about the practical dimensions of daily life in the legal workplaces of America. The women were generous in offering advice and comment, and I would hope that the counsel they offer may be useful to all readers. Most of all, I hope that their stories may be an inspiration to some of the future law students who read these pages.

CAROLE KAMIN BELLOWS

Trial Lawyer; Individual Rights Advocate;
President, Illinois State Bar Association

"I've spent one-third of my life in meetings," says Carole Kamin Bellows. A vivacious, warm individual with a smile that matches her optimistic outlook, she speaks candidly. "The dumbest thing I did in college," she says, "was to elect, one term, to take economics instead of parliamentary procedure . . . which I could have used every day of my life since then." In her junior year, she campaigned for, and won in a contested election, a seat on the Student Senate of the University of Illinois. Since that time, Carole Bellows has been a potent political force wherever she has chosen to apply her talents.

A respected leader in citizens' groups, Mrs. Bellows spent long hours at the podium during the turbulent 1960s. As a member of the Constitutional Convention Committee of the Illinois League of Women Voters, she made speeches throughout the state urging voters to replace an antiquated 1870 document. She was among those who sighed with relief when the Constitution of 1970 was approved by the Illinois electorate.

Although her oldest child was born the year after she was graduated from Northwestern University Law School and two other babies arrived within the next five years, Mrs. Bellows managed to remain active in the practice of law. Working in the law offices of her father and, later, her husband, she has handled a wide variety of cases. Many involve trial work. In more recent years, Carole Bellows has often been at the elbow of female plaintiffs in employment discrimination cases.

As a champion of individual rights, there is perhaps no lawyer in the country with credentials to match those of Carole Kamin Bellows. In her home state, she served for nine years on the Illinois State Bar Association committee on the Bill of Rights, chairing the group during the 1966–67 season. She was editor of the 1970 edition of "Your Bill of Rights," a one-hundred-and-four-page booklet widely distributed to students and teachers throughout the state for use in conjunction with mandated constitutional studies. The publication includes commentary by leading Illinois attorneys on each of some twenty-four key phrases in the first ten Amendments to the United States Constitution. The topics range from "Freedom of the Press" to "Double Jeopardy" to "Compulsory Process." The latter are among the five articles prepared by editor Bellows herself.

In the 1975–76 season, Carole Bellows was Chairman of the powerful American Bar Association's (ABA) Section on Individual Rights and Responsibilities. A member of the Sections' Council since 1967, she has had a variety of other ABA assignments over the years. From the other side of the podium, she has challenged members of the governing body of the ABA—the staid four-hundred-member House of Delegates—to take action on key issues that were often contro-versial. In 1975, she worked hard for passage of a Resolution that would have put the ABA on record as favoring elimina-tion of laws against prostitution. The resolution was defeated by two votes.

In June 1977, Carole Bellows assumed the presidency of the twenty-thousand-member Illinois State Bar Association. It is one of the highest honors that can be conferred by one's professional peers, and it was well deserved. Since 1963, when she was given her first committee role, Carole Bellows has been busy in bar association work at the local, state, and national levels. She is distressed about the young people who do not assume active roles in community and professional groups. A practical person, she says, "No meaningful reforms come about without the support of organized groups." She sees the positions taken by groups such as the organized Bar as significant vehicles for spurring social change. It's an atti-tude that accounts for the hours she has spent in urging par-ticular groups to "take a stand."

In accepting the gavel and leadership of her state Bar, Carole Bellows might well have looked back smugly at the critics of past decades who were saying it couldn't—or shouldn't—be done, that a mother's place was in the home. Instead, she smiled at her three, neatly garbed children sit-ting nearby. Attentive and proud of their mother, they smiled back. Speaking briefly to the group, Mrs. Bellows looked ahead to the issues before the Bar in the coming year.

Backward glancing is not Carole Bellows' style. When questioned, she says she remembers well the atmosphere of the 1950s and 1960s when the working mother was under fire. But she won't discuss the critical comments she fielded from her own doorstep. "I try to forget such things. I know that a person's comments reflect her upbringing and I can appreciate that everyone's background is different." She does laugh, recalling the time she was on an errand with her three children and met a former law professor. "I'll bet you kids are glad to be with your mother for a change," he blurted. Astute Marcia, then about twelve, sprang to her mother's defense, "Oh, we see her all the time."

Carole Bellows says that she always planned to have a career. Though her mother did not practice, both of her parents were lawyers. Did they encourage her to study law? She hesitates. "No," she says, "but it was always expected that I would be in some profession."

Carole Bellows is surrounded by relatives who are lawyers. Her husband and her father-in-law, with whom she is in partnership in the firm of Bellows & Bellows, are Chicago lawyers, as are two uncles. Both of her brothers are lawyers; both are married to the daughters of lawyers. Her father, who is now deceased, practiced law in Chicago for many years. During the 1930s, he served in the office of the Corporation Counsel of the City of Chicago with the fathers-in-law of his sons. One of these men is now a partner in a leading Chicago law firm; the other is a Justice of the Illinois Supreme Court.

Carole Bellows' marriage was, in a sense, contrived in a law office. During the 1950s, her father, Alfred Kamin, and her father-in-law, Charles Bellows, were brought together when working on a major case. Charles heard a lot about Alfred's daughter Carole who was then in law school. Charles says that the first time he met her he knew, "this was the girl for my son Jason." Evidently, he made his views known to the staff. Sometime later, when Carole brought some papers to the office, his secretary invited Jason, who was then practicing in his father's office, to join them for coffee. The wedding took place a year later, in 1958. Today, nearly two decades afterwards, Charles Bellows still raves about his daughter-in-law. "No matter how difficult the situation," he says, "she never becomes disturbed . . . and she never balks at the amount of work put before her."

Despite the legal surroundings in which they were raised, Carole Bellows says that neither she nor her brothers had decided, at an early age, to dedicate themselves to the law. "During high school," she says, "I planned on becoming a doctor. My first two years of college were spent in pre-med studies." When she finally decided that medicine was not for her, she switched to a political science curriculum and pointed herself toward law school.

How does she view this academic background? "The political science was fine," she says. "My only problem was that I did not have an opportunity in the two remaining years after changing my major to take as many history and English courses as I would have liked." Each term, difficult choices (as between economics and parliamentary procedure, for example) had to be made.

Mrs. Bellows doesn't favor any particular major and won't press any special course of study on her daughter, who is planning to be a lawyer. She thinks any academic pursuit is good if it "turns the student on" and compels disciplined use of the mind. She favors courses that demand a lot of reading and writing of many papers.

She says that she was fortunate because her own writing skills were developed early. As an editor and active reporter on the high school paper, she gained valuable practical experience in writing. She also feels that Evanston High School, which she attended, offered superior instruction in journalism.

Like many highly successful people, Carole Bellows has the ability to do several things at once. In her bright blue carpeted office, she often stands while talking on the telephone. While talking, she moves about to organize the papers on her desk, sorting and making notes. Without a pause in the conversation with her client, she smiles at a visitor who enters the office. Infrequently, she turns to gaze out the broad window that offers a postcard view of Lake Michigan and the Chicago River.

Today, Carole Bellows is an expert speaker. She delivers clearly and forcefully messages larded with lively anecdotes. She is adept at establishing rapport with her audience. However, this was not always so. Mrs. Bellows confesses that she was somewhat shy during her high school years. Now a seasoned campaigner, she says she never ran for anything or did any public speaking until her junior year of college.

"That was a turning point," she explains. "Free of the lab and science courses of pre-med, I had more time. I became very active in the Women's Group System (WGS), an organization of independent (nonsorority) women on campus." She recalls that the experience of winning the Senate seat was "fantastic" because it involved speaking to countless campus groups in all kinds of circumstances. It led to an enthusiasm for politics that has been with her ever since.

The campus campaigner was not the shy girl from Evanston High. Where had the confidence come from? Mrs. Bellows gives some share of the credit to an unusual job she had during the summer following graduation from high school. A skilled swimmer, Carole Kamin was one of a troop of all-female lifeguards who policed the shores at Wilmette Beach on Lake Michigan in the summer of 1953. "We kept in shape by rowing two miles a day. We controlled the whole beach and were responsible for the safety of scores of bathers who came to this beach every day. It had a tremendous impact in helping me to build confidence and leadership ability," she says.

She recalls that a news story was written about the all-girl squad that year. The practice of hiring girls was a holdover from World War II days. In 1954, it was abandoned. Males were hired and the girls were out of jobs. Carole Bellows believes that the incident may have had something to do with her subsequent heavy involvement in sex discrimination litigation. For the past several years, such matters have occupied nearly half of the time she has spent in private practice. On behalf of female plaintiffs, she has pressed for enforcement of both state and federal laws including the Equal Pay Act of 1963, Title VII of the Civil Rights Act of 1964, and Title IX of the Education Amendments of 1972.

Two recent cases brought Mrs. Bellows before hearing examiners of the Illinois Fair Employment Practice Commission to make arguments on behalf of teachers. One case involved a female professor at a local college who had been denied tenure and promotion in spite of having outstanding qualifications. In the other case, the complainant was an elementary school teacher who charged sex discrimination in hiring by a district that had advertised for a "male" teacher for third grade.

Carole Bellows' work requires conferences with employers and with the bureaucrats charged with enforcement responsibilities in a host of government agencies. Nearly every case involves the writing of letters, memoranda, requests for hearings, and petitions for relief of all kinds.

At least twice a week, Carole Bellows can be found in the hallways of the Federal Building or in the courtrooms of the Daley Center in the Chicago Loop. On occasion, she appears before the U.S. Court of Appeals for the Seventh Circuit, the body that hears appeals from court decisions in Illinois, Indiana, and Wisconsin. Here, in an elegant courtroom the size of a school gym, three or more of the current Justices preside.

It is clear that Carole Bellows is at home and fully at ease in all of the courtrooms of Chicago. She says that she is troubled by something she does *not* see in many of the courtrooms she visits—women lawyers arguing the cases. "Of course, there are some women in litigation," she says, "but I don't see as many of them as I would like to."

She isn't sure of the reason for the lack of female litigators. She does feel strongly that no branches of law are especially appropriate for women and, conversely, that none should be closed to them. She knows that there have been few women in corporate practice or serving as general counsels of major corporations. But she expects this to change. "I think that business is now actively seeking female legal talent. I believe women will move into the corporate world rapidly." Do women have to work harder? "Yes," she says without hesitation. Will this always be true? "Probably for twenty years," she replies, "at least until all the children raised in traditional households are grown up."

She hopes that women will enter all fields of the law. Moreover, she believes that they should make their moves right after law school. She has two bits of advice for young female law graduates. One, do not "drop out," even temporarily; two, think very carefully before hanging out a shingle to practice alone.

Carole Bellows worries about the lawyer (male or female) who is fresh out of law school and attempting to practice alone. "When you are graduated from law school," she says, "you are really not ready to take on the responsibilities a law practice requires. Passing the Bar is not enough. You should be exposed to many situations with experienced people present to tutor you." She views as essential some period of internship, when the young lawyer has access to the advice of seasoned attorneys.

In emphasizing this concern, she makes clear that she is talking not only about substantive decisions, but also about the fine points of procedure. She notes that these are often the hardest bits of information to secure independently. She recalls a couple of recent occasions when young women who practice alone called her about difficulties. "One of them," she says, "fouled up on an appeal. If she had been in a firm, an experienced associate could have quickly set her straight."

She knows that women with babies or young children often have difficulties in finding help that would make it possible for them to meet the 9 A.M. to 5 P.M. (or later) commitment required by law firms and businesses. It is tempting for them to try, instead, to practice from offices that are physically located in or very near to their homes and apartments. It is this kind of solitary practice that worries Mrs. Bellows. An experienced lawyer, she is well aware that even a small mistake can seriously jeopardize a client's position. She also feels that it is definitely preferable to maintain an office *outside of* one's home.

What then are the options for women law graduates who have young children? One suggestion Mrs. Bellows offers to women who have opportunities for good positions with large urban firms is that they find housing nearby. As a life-long suburbanite, she knows what she is talking about. She says, "The time wasted in commuting is just enormous. Also, when you live twenty miles away it is not feasible to go back to the office after the kids are in bed at night."

One alternative that Mrs. Bellows never recommends to

young mothers is retiring, even temporarily. She feels it is very important to keep one's hand in the profession in some way. Her own lawyer-mother was active in community affairs but did not work outside the home. Carole Bellows says that she always knew that this life-style was not for her. "I could never stay home full time," she says, "I couldn't handle that . . . psychologically or emotionally." At the same time, she confesses that she did not make long-range career plans. "I'm the kind of person who takes each day as it comes," she says. "I'm more likely to worry about who will take care of the baby tomorrow than what I'll be doing ten years from now. I don't worry about things unless they are on top of me."

Despite the alleged absence of plan, the steps in Carole Bellows' career follow a logical sequence. Since that September day in 1960 when she was notified that she had passed the Illinois Bar, she kept active in the practice of law. In 1972, she joined her father-in-law and husband in the firm of Bellows & Bellows. She describes it as a "litigation-oriented" office that handles a variety of cases. As a young assistant state's attorney, Charles Bellows traveled to Greece to bring back to the United States the famed public utilities magnate, Sam Insull. Charles Bellows made his name as a criminal lawyer, but he handles other legal problems as well.

His son Jason, who was graduated from the University of Chicago Law School in 1956, is quiet in demeanor. But he is an enthusiastic booster of all of Carole's professional endeavors. Over the years, he has been willing to lend a hand at home. Carole calls her husband's supportive role "absolutely essential." "I have made such a time commitment," she confesses, "I simply couldn't do it all without him."

Discussing the problems of combining a career and family,

she cites the example of a female friend in Washington who is working for a law firm while her husband, who is writing a book, takes care of the baby. She says, "One thing that is going to have to change in society as a whole . . . and I am seeing this more and more . . . is that the other parent is going to have to take more of the responsibility at home."

In 1962, Mrs. Bellows began what was to be a ten-year stint assisting Chief Justice Maurice Perlin of the Illinois Court of Claims. Fortunately, this work was not full time and did not interfere too much with her practice. Nor did it have to be done in a structured setting. She could bring work home, and she did not have to be at the office for fixed hours. It was an interesting job. Both contract and tort (civil action) claims against the state of Illinois come before this court. The initial proceedings in such cases are conducted by hearing officers. Mrs. Bellows' task was to aid the Judge in considering the records and in writing opinions in the cases reviewed by the court. She views the experience as useful, but she adds, "There is really nothing that is equivalent to practicing law."

During the 1960s, Carole Bellows worked hard persuading Illinois citizens to convene a constitutional convention. At the convention, she testified before the Bill of Rights subcommittee. Many of the issues were complicated and her legal training was clearly helpful. Does she view this experience as valuable? She does not discount it. Neither does she strongly recommend it. "I can't say that I regret it because I never look back . . . if I can't do something about a matter, I don't think about it." All the same, one senses some small remorse for the hours expended in activities of this kind. "It is not the same as practicing law," she says, "and it is much more time-consuming in its own way." She notes too the danger in getting enmeshed in volunteer work and never moving on to a full professional commitment. She feels legal aid work can be useful, for a time. She notes, with some chagrin, that one acquaintance of hers has been doing part-time work of this sort for twenty years.

In 1977, Carole Bellows served on a special screening committee appointed to assess qualifications and make recommendations concerning candidates to Illinois Supreme Court Justices. The Justices were responsible for filling certain judicial posts in the state court system. At the same time, she herself was on the list of candidates being considered by U.S. Senator Adlai Stevenson for appointment to federal judgeships. Carole Bellows says that attaining a judgeship is not one of her career goals. But she readily admits that she would find it hard to turn down an opportunity to serve on the federal bench.

Carole Bellows sees herself—and says she always has—as a lawyer wholly devoted to the profession. She winces at the term "part-time," as used to describe her own legal work in the early 1960s. However, she does admit that she was at home more during the years when her children were born— Marcia in 1961, Douglas in 1963, and Daniel in 1966. She has strong views about the rearing of very young children. "Up to about age four," she says, "children need a great deal of very consistent attention." Older children, she feels, can benefit by helping with housework themselves. She recalls that Daniel, at age eight, did the family washing during one period when she was looking for a housekeeper. Her mother, who died in 1973, was also extremely helpful.

For some years, Mrs. Bellows has had a housekeeper who comes in around 10:30 A.M. and stays until 5:30 P.M. She says that she and her husband are seldom home by that hour, but she finds that the children manage nicely. "Having three color television sets reduces the arguments," says Jason. On week nights, the children sometimes start dinner. Jason cooks too, often preparing gourmet meals on Sundays. Carole estimates that she does about 75 percent of the cooking.

For Carole, Saturday work has been routine. Often, it involves attending meetings of Bar committees. During the early part of 1977, she devoted more than twenty hours a week solely to the task of appointing nearly 800 Illinois lawyers to the dozens of standing committees of the state Bar. During 1977, the year Carole Bellows took the reins of the Illinois Bar, she spent at least sixty hours a week on work outside the home. However, she says that she does not usually bring heavy briefcases home now as she did in the early days of her practice. In recent years, she has tried to keep the hours at the house in Wilmette free for other tasks. Of course, work-related telephone calls occupy many hours, even on weekends.

Carole Bellows is comfortable in delegating many household tasks to others. She says she is not overly concerned with the house itself and is willing to delegate anything "that does not have to do directly with the children." Nowadays, her helper drives, but she admits that transportation for the children can be a hassle. She confesses that on more than one occasion she has missed important meetings to meet car pool obligations. She doesn't consider P.T.A. a "children's activity," but she tries to attend all school functions in which her children are participating. She and another working mother are sometimes the only moms in attendance at basketball games scheduled at 8:30 A.M. on Saturdays.

This is not to suggest that Carole Bellows is an early riser. To the contrary, she claims that she is a "night person," late to bed, and struggling to get up in the morning. She is up to say good-bye, but seldom breakfasts with the children, who fix their own meal before departing for school each day.

When Carole must travel, which is often, Jason is there with the children. Sometimes, the children go along. Since 1973, the entire family has gone to the annual American Bar Association meetings in August. The children participate in supervised young people's activities. In March 1977, Carole and three other Illinois Bar representatives spent a few days in Washington on the annual visit with members of the Illinois delegation to Congress. The trip coincided with a school holiday. Jason and the children toured Washington while Carole was on Capitol Hill. Afterwards, the family headed for Williamsburg.

All of the Bellows children are interested in music. For Carole, this has meant attending many concerts and endless chauffering for lessons. Douglas plays the guitar, violin, and clarinet and has taken music lessons of one sort or another since he was in fourth grade. Daniel also likes sports. His games and practices bring more driving chores. Marcia is interested in drama. She won a small role in a 1977 production of "A Midsummer Night's Dream" at New Trier West High School, where she is an honor student. A specialist in chocolate chip cookies, she enjoys baking.

Mrs. Bellows recalls that when he was younger, Daniel would sometimes fret about her going to the office. "Mommy, do you have to go downtown today?" She chuckles, "But he is my baby . . . he would like one hundred percent of my attention all of the time." All of the children have gone to the office with their parents often.

Marcia recalls that during her elementary school years, she was surprised to learn that the mothers of many of her friends did not work. She says that instead of being unhappy, she felt superior about her mother's different occupation.

She is interested in women's rights issues and would like to be a lawyer. She also feels that she would want a family. Does she see any problems in having both career and family? She smiles and talks about her busy relatives. "I think it will work out," she says.

Does Carole encourage her daughter or other friends to go to law school? She says she will be delighted if Marcia becomes a lawyer, but she won't push. "I will encourage my children in anything they want to do if it is constructive," she says. However, she knows something of the huge numbers of students being graduated from law school. She feels that, even if the expected expansion of legal jobs develops, many will have trouble finding employment in the profession. "I don't think that mediocre students should go to law school these days," she says.

She feels that the future for bright women who study law is secure. She sees the opportunities developing rapidly. But she cautions that in moving into an essentially male world, women must "act professionally." What does the phrase mean to Carole Bellows? She feels it stems from an internalized image of oneself. In professional contacts, it means thinking, "I am a lawyer and that is why I am here." She emphasizes that it also means that she does not think of herself as a "lady-lawyer." She doesn't discuss domestic issues at work. She says that a woman who goes into a firm and then lunches only with female secretaries misses "the essential part of being a lawyer." To Carole Bellows, this means, "Being one of the guys and talking business." She emphasizes that this is a vital part of legal internship. She admits that she spends much of her time, even at cocktail parties, talking business with men.

Slim, modishly dressed, and sporting a fashionably curly

hairdo, Carole Bellows is an attractive woman. She clearly
has a faculty, too, for putting men (and women) of all ages
at ease. She confesses that she has taken some potshots over
the years from hostile practitioners who probably thought
she should be at home. How does she deal with them? "With
humor," she says. "If you react or let this penetrate, you are
losing the game."

In spite of her frantic schedule, Carole Bellows is the
kind of person who "takes time" for people. She is unfail-
ingly considerate. If she must excuse herself, she finds a
newspaper for the visitor to read until her return.

She is also a disciplined worker who seldom requires
overtime of staff. Her secretary reports that whatever the
demands of her schedule, she appears relaxed and displays
an almost total lack of temperament. Returning to her desk
after a business trip, the pile of pink slips noting phone calls
to be returned is thick. She spreads them out and, selecting
the most pressing ones, begins. Greetings to clients are warm
and mostly on a first-name basis. Despite the press of time,
there is no urgency in her voice. When she spills a cup of
tea over the whole lot, there is no panic. She simply wipes
the batch off and carefully clips the soggier papers onto the
radiator to dry.

In arguing a case before the court, she displays the same
pleasant, even-handed demeanor. Her thoughtful presentation reflects careful preparation. Afterwards, there is a cordial exchange with opposing counsel.

As President of the Illinois Bar, as Chairman of a major
Section of the ABA, and as a busy practitioner, Carole Bellows presents a highly favorable personal and professional
image. From the podium, she charms audiences. In one-to-
one contacts, she comes through as a concerned person and
a competent lawyer. It is an image that is helpful to women

lawyers everywhere. She has already done much to build respect for women in the profession. Given her skill, her position, and her commitment, it is certain that Carole Bellows will continue to serve as an attractive, articulate advocate for all women in the working world for years to come.

MARY STALLINGS COLEMAN

Former Judge, Juvenile Court; Justice of the Supreme Court of Michigan

Justice Mary Stallings Coleman had an inducement to enter the legal profession that few lawyers, of either sex, can match. She was encouraged to study law by one of the most famous Justices ever to serve on the United States Supreme Court, the late Oliver Wendell Holmes, Jr. As a shy teenager, she confessed to him that she was thinking of becoming a lawyer. Enthusiastic, Justice Holmes responded that, in his view, the legal profession needed more women

A student at Washington, D.C.'s McKinley High School, an awed Mary Stallings had been prodded by her mother to request the interview with the elderly Justice. The objective? To get firsthand material for an oratorical contest in which Mary had been assigned the topic, "Oliver Wendell Holmes: The Great Dissenter." Mary came away from the meeting with Holmes' hearty approval—a dividend that would help carry her through the long, exhausting years when she worked her way through George Washington Law

School in the nation's capital. She also came away from the interview with enough choice quotes to win second place in the city-wide contest. Afterwards, she recalls that one of the judges confided to her, "If you had been a boy, you would have had first place."

Due to the contest experience, Mary became more aware of her own talents, of the opportunities ahead in law, and, finally, of the reality of the sex bias she might face.

Today, she readily acknowledges that the bias exists, and that it did exist during the long years of her move up the legal ladder from attorney in the Lands Division of the U.S. Department of Agriculture to sit as the first woman ever on the Supreme Court of Michigan. She claims though that she has been lucky, that sex discrimination seldom touched her or held her back. She says she rarely felt bias, not during the days when, as a young mother, she practiced law in Washington, D.C., and in Battle Creek, Michigan, nor during the twelve years she served as a juvenile court judge. Both of her daughters, now grown and married, are physicians. She says that neither she nor her husband hesitated in encouraging the girls to enter the male-dominated medical profession.

The visitor who talks to Mary Coleman today sees the merest hint of the timid Holmes interviewer in the Justice's quiet manner and in the spacing of the smiles between her soft-spoken responses. On the other hand, as she walks along the shopping mall in the middle of Battle Creek, her adopted hometown, the trim-figured, dark-haired Justice greets acquaintances every few paces. Striding purposefully to her appointment, she talks of these faces and the events of her years in Battle Creek. The warm, considerate, concerned human being shows through. It is clear, too, that the self-confidence runs deep now. The visitor begins to reconcile the image of the sensitive girl with that of the skilled politician, which the mature Mary Stallings Coleman so definitely is.

She earned her place on Michigan's highest court in an arduous state-wide campaign. Supreme court seats are coveted posts. In Michigan, over the years they have been sought (and won) by many ex-governors and other political powers whose faces were already familiar to voters across the state. In 1972, when Mary Coleman ran for the eight-year term, a field of nine candidates was competing for two seats on the high court.

There were many hurdles for Mary to clear. The Michigan system for electing supreme court justices is unusual. Candidates must be nominated by a political party, but afterwards they run independently as nonpartisans. Candidates' ties to party (and, more important, to party funds) are severed. In Mary Coleman's case, the drive for her nomination came late and her campaign was hastily put together.

Mary had served with distinction as President of the Michigan Probate and Juvenile Judges Association during the 1971–72 term. At their August meeting in 1972, sentiment for her candidacy for a seat on the court mushroomed. Unfortunately, the Republican convention, from which her nomination would have to come, was set for early September —just weeks away.

However, once the idea was out, there was a ground swell of support. Loyal local printers stopped their presses. They set aside local orders and began to grind out thousands of bright yellow "sunshine" faces, for Mary's supporters to wear. The tags bore the simple message, "Nominate Judge Mary," with the name printed atop the wide smile on each face. Pretty young boosters, who became known as Judge Mary's "sunshine girls," distributed the tags. The deluge of sunshine, coupled with Mary Coleman's reputation as an experienced judge, brought the nomination at the convention.

Vital as it was, the nomination was more of a beginning than an end. Ahead was a campaign circuit that would thrust Mary Coleman in a nonstop orbit of ever-widening circles around the state. Funds for the entire effort had to be raised. Under Michigan law, the party cord had been cut. Requests for contributions had to be made independently. Those in the Coleman camp were hampered by the late start; there had been earlier callers at many promising doors. The zeal of the Judge's supporters made the difference.

Local talent produced beautiful picture postcards for the Judge's supporters to mail to friends. Youthful Coleman workers handed out tiny game schedules containing the Judge's picture to voters in the huge crowds at the University of Michigan and Michigan State football games in the fall of 1972. Delighted at the prospect of having such an experienced colleague on the state's highest court, many trial judges rolled up their sleeves to help.

Mary Coleman took time to visit with local newspeople everywhere. In the end, she received an unprecedented thirty-eight out of forty endorsements made by major news media in Michigan. There were other firsts. Mary Coleman had been the first woman to be nominated; she was the first to win. For the first time ever, the Michigan Bar distributed straw ballots to its more than twelve thousand members. Mary received the largest number of lawyers' votes.

At the wheel day and night that autumn, driving Mary to and through the cities and towns of the Wolverine state, was Judge Creighton R. Coleman, Mary's husband. She flatly states that Creighton Coleman was, in fact, responsible for it all. "He is, was, and always has been, my strongest supporter," she says emphatically. When the pressure came from the Judges' Association for her candidacy, Creighton urged her on. Would she have undertaken the campaign had he felt otherwise? There is no hesitation in her negative reply. She views the role of her supportive spouse as all-important in the success of all that she has undertaken. "I believe," she says, "that it would be very difficult for anyone to combine a career and family without an enthusiastic and helpful spouse." Over the years, Creighton Coleman has been both. A very successful lawyer in his own right, Judge Creighton Coleman now sits on the Circuit Court bench in Marshall, Michigan. Located ten miles from Battle Creek, Marshall is a community of palatial homes and the county seat of Calhoun County.

Creighton grew up in Calhoun County and was graduated from the University of Michigan. However, he migrated to Washington, D.C., for legal training and work with the U.S. government. A fellow student at George Washington University Law School, he says he literally dropped his books when he saw Mary enter the law library one evening. He proposed just a month later. They were married the following year, a few days after Mary's graduation.

Graduation for Mary was the culmination of four years of unbelievably hard work and more than a decade of dreaming. She says that, as a little girl, she began telling people that she wanted to be a lawyer. Laughingly, she says that maybe sheer repetition of this childhood response brought about her final decision to study law. She also admits that it may have come because her father was a lawyer, and her mother, though not a member of the Bar, qualified (under then-existing rules) to hold a number of key legal positions in the U.S. Department of Justice. Agnes Stallings had a distinguished career in government service. In fact, in the 1930s, it was reported that Eleanor Roosevelt had suggested Agnes Stallings as one of four *women* that President Roosevelt should consider in filling vacancies on the U.S. Supreme Court.

Justice Coleman's parents met at the University of Texas. Both were students at the time, but her mother dropped out of college when they were married. Her father practiced law in Texas for a time. When Mary was four years old, the Stallings moved to Washington, D.C.

Agnes Stallings "learned the law" in the old-fashioned way, by working in her husband's law offices in Texas and in Washington, D.C. When Mary was ten years old, her father became ill, and he was an invalid until his death, seven years later. Not long after he became ill, Agnes Stallings went to work full time.

Mary's grandmother lived in the home and was able to care for Mary, an only child. Still, Agnes Stallings had a substantial burden. Doctors' bills were enormous; extensive nursing care had to be provided. There was no extra money and precious little extra time. "Looking back," says Mary, "I do not see how she managed. Incredibly, she also entertained for me. On Sunday nights, we had open houses . . . my friends were welcome for creamed chicken or waffles. She always made do, no matter how many came." Mary says that in later years, when she herself was juggling a growing law practice and her own children's activities, she often thought of her mother's efforts.

Agnes Stallings faced other challenges that were unique— and frightening. Serving in the U.S. Department of Justice at the time of Prohibition, Agnes Stallings was Chief of the section responsible for enforcement of the beer and wine provisions of the Volstead Act. Threats of physical harm to herself and to her daughter were frequent. Mary recalls one episode when a rock was hurled at her bedroom window, smashing the glass and knocking over a lamp on her desk. On another occasion, Mary was sent away to Chesapeake Bay for a short time after a threatening note had been slipped under the Stallings' back door.

Like many good students of that day, Mary had skipped grades, and she was graduated from high school at age sixteen. The following fall, she entered the University of Maryland. Mary Coleman says she has been heavily involved in civic activities all of her life. It was no less true during her years at the university. Assistant editor of the college magazine, she was also active in theater work and in her sorority, Alpha Omicron Pi. As a senior, she was selected for membership in the local chapter of Mortar Board, the national honorary society for outstanding senior college students.

Years later, in May of 1978, she was awarded the honorary degree of Doctor of Laws by her alma mater. As a student leader, Mary was often called upon to escort visiting dignitaries around the campus. She recalls that on one occasion when she was in charge of a campus dance, she was asked to entertain a visiting senator on the same evening. She laughs, "We all went to the dance . . . me, my date, and Senator Ratcliffe." Later, Senator Ratcliffe would recommend Mary for a teaching position in one of Maryland's premier districts. Without changing her plan to study law, Mary had decided, midway through college, to obtain a teaching certificate. Her thought was that she could teach for a time and earn the money needed for law school. Throughout college, she earned money by grading papers and doing other chores in the college office. During her senior year, she earned welcome dollars as a substitute teacher. As it turned out, she did not take a teaching position on graduation. Instead, she was able to get a government position in

Washington, D.C., that permitted her to enroll in law school immediately.

At George Washington Law School, she completed four years of work in three, following an exhausting schedule. Each day she worked from 8 A.M. to 4 P.M., and then rushed to Law School for classes that began at 4:30 P.M. Often, she did not eat her evening meal until 9 P.M. Studies had to be completed after that.

As an undergraduate, she had majored in English and modern languages. She found that these studies were an almost ideal preparation for law school. "I recommend a major in English to any young person who is planning a legal career. Because most of the lawyer's time is spent speaking or writing . . . verbal skill is essential."

As a Justice on the Michigan Supreme Court, Mary Coleman writes about fifty opinions a year. It is a vital part of her work, but the volume is small compared to the mountains of other communications that have always gone out from her office. In the years of her practice there were briefs and motions to be prepared and oral arguments to be outlined. Nowadays, there are memoranda, recommendations, and letters beyond count—many related to juvenile law, an area in which she has special interest and experience.

As an experienced Juvenile Court Judge, and before that, as a Referee, she has long been deeply concerned with legislation that involves the treatment of juveniles. A drafter of many key provisions in the Michigan Code, she feels that proposals for reform must be carefully weighed. If she feels a revision is ill-considered, she doesn't simply chafe and mutter. Instead, she prepares position papers spotlighting weaknesses and distributes them to legislators and colleagues. She has, on many occasions, testified before legislative committees.

Mary Coleman is a doer. An articulate advocate, she is also a good listener. She recalls that when she was in private practice, and alone in the Battle Creek office one morning, a man came in about a divorce. Told that her husband would not be in that day, he said he would return because he couldn't tell *her* the full story. Not pressing the man, but chatting easily, Mary Coleman was soon listening calmly as he recited all the lurid details.

Mary Coleman presents an extremely chic, feminine appearance. Her manner inspires trust, on both the personal and professional levels. Judge Wendell L. Scoder, a Calhoun County colleague, recalls the time he thoughtlessly delivered a blast against female lawyers one day while riding with a group of lawyers to a funeral. Reminded that an embarrassed Mary was present in the back seat of the car at the time, he compounded his gaffe by saying that he never thought of Mary as a woman. Both laugh about the incident today.

Mary Coleman long ago earned the respect of members of the local Bar. And her reputation traveled. She was, at one time, the only female attorney employed as local counsel by the New York Central Railroad. For a number of years, she was the only woman to attend the annual informational meetings in New York that were arranged by the general counsel of the railroad.

For more than a decade, Mary played the leading role in the Battle Creek firm of Wunsch & Coleman. The other partners of the firm, which was founded when the Colemans settled there a few years after World War II, were her husband and Ernest Wunsch. A prominent Detroit lawyer, Wunsch helped to establish the firm because he intended eventually to leave Detroit and pursue a quieter life in nearby Marshall. As it happened, he died before retiring to Marshall and spent little time in the Battle Creek office.

Creighton Coleman's responsibilities outside of Battle Creek were also substantial. Shortly after the Colemans returned to Michigan in 1948, a group of local citizens persuaded him to run for the state Senate. He won that election, and several thereafter, spending eight years as a legislator in Lansing.

At first, Creighton commuted from Battle Creek to Lansing, driving 120 miles each weekday when the legislature was in session. As assignments increased, it became necessary for him to stay in Lansing from Monday through Thursday many weeks. Meantime, the Battle Creek practice was growing. Mary was busy with the children and a host of civic activities, but she began tending to more and more matters at the office. When she was admitted to the Michigan Bar in 1950, their youngest daughter, Carole, was about to enter kindergarten. Creighton asked his wife if she would consider assuming a full partnership in the firm. She readily agreed.

Mary Coleman had heavy responsibilities at the law office. There were no live-in relatives to help her with tasks at home, as her own grandmother had done when her mother was at work. How did she manage? "When you have your own office," she says, "you can exercise a bit more control over your schedule." She recalls that most days she tried to be home by about 4 P.M. If she were going to be delayed, she would call on one of the reliable women on her list to fill in for her at home. There was help with the laundry and cleaning. All the same, days were long. Mary spent the day at the office and returned home in the late afternoon to prepare dinner and be with the children. Each night, after they were in bed, she opened her briefcase to finish work brought home from the office.

Her older daughter Leslie, now married and herself a busy physician and mother of three small children, wonders how her mother did it. She recalls that her mother was often a "room mother" at school, and that she was constantly called upon to drive the girls to various activities. Looking back, Mary remembers the chauffeuring duties as among the most difficult to arrange. She muses that perhaps she was called upon too much. She recalls discussing this once with an experienced teacher. The teacher told her that she had noticed that the children of working mothers were quicker to volunteer parents for driving and other chores. "Is it because they want to show that their mother *can* do it?" she had wondered aloud. The same teacher had wryly observed that nonworking mothers seemed to be less reluctant to refuse such chores.

Mary's conscientious attention to maternal duties was not lost on the girls. Leslie says she cannot recall any occasion when her mother did not take her turn or could not come to a school event. Mary herself remembers some juggling. "Many times I was glad that I had my own office," she says, "it meant I could arrange to leave for a half hour to take cupcakes over to school, for example." She recalls that once she asked the judge and opposing counsel to put a case off to the next day because Leslie was in a school play. "I knew that she would be disappointed if I could not be there," she confides. She says such direct conflicts were rare, but she rates the scheduling as the most challenging chore during those years.

Both girls began helping with housework when they were quite young. Creighton, when he was there, pitched in too. He had no hang-ups about "women's work." Leslie recalls that he nearly always helped with the dishes after dinner and often did the grocery shopping. A good shopper, he has for years bought most of Mary's clothes. Looking over her present wardrobe, she estimates that he selected about 90 percent of the items in her closet.

Concerned about Mary's overworking, he monitors her activities. For years, he has battled to get her to curb her late-night "legal homework" and get more sleep. Some years back, he grew concerned about the growing number of speaking engagements on her calendar. He extracted a promise from her that she would limit herself to no more than 100 speeches a year, or an average of about two a week. She now tries to adhere to this pledge.

None of Creighton's concern stems from doubting Mary's abilities. It comes rather from a genuine appreciation of her talent, and the fear that others will impose upon her because of it. "As an actress or a speaker," he says, "she can charm any audience." Obviously, those who come and hear her agree, and tell others. Each year, many requests to speak must be refused.

Listening to the popular speaker, it is difficult to believe that she was shy as a youngster. Justice Coleman says that her interest in drama was the bridge. Both in high school and in college, she appeared in school productions. In Battle Creek, she helped to found a theater group and often appeared there in leading roles. Creighton recalls that local critics raved about her performance in "The Heiress," terming it "better than Broadway." Mary says these experiences on the stage have helped her immeasurably in handling the verbal chores that have fallen to her as a practicing lawyer and as a judge.

There were plenty of those chores in her twelve years in the juvenile courtroom. Continuously, in chambers and in the courtroom, she was called upon to deliver messages of the utmost delicacy and importance to persons from every segment of society in Calhoun County. Sometimes, it took considerable courage to communicate with the clientele of the Court. On a few occasions, after fruitless forays by court officials, Judge Coleman went directly to the homes of juveniles. Once she managed, where others had failed, to persuade a near-incompetent grandmother to allow the grandson she had sequestered to move to a foster home and attend school. Stern responses were sometimes required too. Mary recalls calling to her chambers a young juvenile who had telephoned her home the previous evening and threatened her daughter. She warned him in severest tones never to do that again.

Mary Coleman confesses that she had a special interest in young people long before her years in Juvenile Court. When Creighton was an attorney in the Anti-Trust Division of the Department of Justice, she traveled with him to New York and other cities on the East Coast. Often, she visited the juvenile or family courts. When Creighton's transfer to New York seemed imminent, she applied for admission to the School of Social Work of Columbia University. She felt that this training, with her law degree, would give her special skill in working with juveniles. The war came, and she did not enroll. But years later, when the opportunity arose, Mary Coleman jumped at the chance to serve in the local juvenile court.

Both Mary and Creighton have devoted thousands of hours to public service. It appears that a good share of their motivation for accepting such assignments (both paid and unpaid) stemmed from their experiences in Germany following World War II.

During World War II, Creighton served as a naval officer,

doing intelligence work in Washington and, later, in Germany. At the end of the war, he was "civilianized," but remained in Germany with the occupation forces. He served for a time as Ambassador Murphy's advisor on cartels. Later, he was on the staff of General Lucius Clay and a part of the Quadripartite Commission that governed Berlin. He devoted much time to work on "decartelization" measures that were designed to break up the corporate giants that had dominated German industry.

Immediately after the end of the war, Mary and toddler Leslie, aged three, joined him in Berlin. The family lived in a repaired German home in the devastated city. Mary recalls vividly the ruin that was Berlin in 1946. The rubble was piled high in every part of the town. Streets were massive ruts, the paving reduced to fragments. The most common necessities had to be flown in. Before the trip, Mary's planning and foresight had been put to a severe test. She brought baby food, diapers, powdered milk, and shoes for the girls in graduated sizes.

Not long after Mary arrived, there was a highly unusual happening in the grim military hospital near the Coleman quarters. Infant Carole Coleman arrived. She was the first American baby born in Berlin after the war. Her birth brought joy to the hospital's entire patient population. "It was an event!" says Mary, "Many of the gruffest, bearded men stopped to see the baby. The braver ones asked me if they could hold her for a while."

Mary Coleman's years as a mother and wife in post-war Berlin were challenging and hardly those of a typical housewife. But when the time came to sign on for another two-year stint, the Colemans decided it was time to head home. Their decision was hastened by the crisis that brought the Berlin airlift and orders for Mary and the children to leave the troubled town. Creighton had had several offers for jobs back in the states. On her arrival home, Mary checked out some of them. In the end, they decided they would be happiest back in Michigan. When the chance for Creighton to run for office came so soon after they arrived, they were doubly pleased with their decision.

"Seeing what had happened in Germany," says Mary, "we resolved that we would do our best to contribute to public life and work in whatever ways we could to insure that this could not happen in our own country."

Thus it was that Creighton put in so many years in the Michigan legislature for compensation then far below that which he could have commanded for his hours elsewhere. (Mary recalls that his beginning salary was $2,400 per year.) Not too many years after his retirement from the legislature, the opportunity came for Mary to enter government service, and she responded with equal enthusiasm.

Again, Creighton was a behind-the-scenes booster. It was he who found out about the plan of the local judge to appoint a "Referee" to help with juvenile court matters. In Michigan, juvenile and probate work is administered through the same court system. In larger cities, the work is divided and the judges tend to handle one or the other. In less populous areas, such as Calhoun County, one judge handles both dockets. Sometime during 1960, Creighton had lunch with the man then serving as Judge of the local Probate and Juvenile Court. He complained about the burgeoning workload, and particularly about the heavy increase in the juvenile work which he did not enjoy. Finding a Referee to relieve him of many of the chores related to the juvenile cases seemed an ideal solution. Creighton thought Mary was the ideal person to fill this slot.

He urged her to consider it. It was a position a lot of

spouses might not have taken, under the circumstances. Mary had been carrying a full load at the office. In the small firm, this could mean nothing for Creighton but a huge increase in his own workload. But he knew of Mary's long-time interest in juveniles. He knew that she would be tempted to take this position. She was, and she did. She served for nearly a year as Referee. The following year, the sitting Judge retired and Mary ran for election to the judge-ship. There was opposition that first time. In the two subsequent elections for this post, she ran unopposed. Her reputation as an outstanding Judge was growing.

Talking with her about young people and their problems, it is easy to see why she was so successful. "With young people," she says, "it is of upmost importance to be very fair. If they feel that they have been treated unfairly, you lose them." Mary Coleman worked long hours to avoid losing any of the juveniles who came into her courtroom. At one point, she helped to design and furnish a special courtroom for them. She explains the problem. "When I first began this work," she says, "there was a theory that we should carry informality to the limit, even to having everyone—lawyers, parents, juvenile, judge—sit around an ordinary conference table. It wasn't satisfactory. Even the kids complained. They said they wanted to be treated like adults, to go to a regular courtroom. On the other hand, when we used the regular courtroom, the high bench seemed remote and the proceedings became too stiff."

Judge Coleman's solution was a lower, curved bench that stands about three feet high at the sides, and just under four feet at the center in front of the chair from which the judge presides. Curved counsel tables stand on each side of the courtroom, all in the same warm brown walnut with which the room is paneled. Juveniles standing in front of the bench look directly into the eyes of the judge. There is a coziness about the room, but formality and authority are evident too. It is an atmosphere that suits the Judge well and mirrors the special style that brought her success, too, as a member of the top court in her state. In her case, it is literally true that she has progressed from the "lowest" bench in Michigan to the highest one.

In Lansing, Justice Coleman uses elegant quarters in the Law Building and is aided by two law clerks. They assist with research and the writing of opinions. She confesses that they also help her keep abreast of new developments in the law by reading materials and extracting pertinent items.

At her side each day in Lansing or in the smaller, green-carpeted suite the court maintains for her in Battle Creek is her secretary of eighteen years, Edith Hardesty. Their relationship is warm and laced with mutual respect. The Justice says that Mrs. Hardesty cheerfully does the work of three ordinary people. Mrs. Hardesty's appraisal of Justice Coleman is much the same. Over the years, there have been thousands of shared hours. When the Justice must be in Lansing, which is a few days each week and every day at least one week a month, Mrs. Hardesty and Justice Coleman often commute together. The only exceptions are nights when Mrs. Hardesty must get home early to go bowling.

Justice Coleman does not bowl, or golf, or play tennis. In the summer, she sometimes swims, but she says she has little time for recreation. She still brings work home and most nights she prepares dinner that she and Creighton enjoy, often with wine and candlelight, in the lovely dining room of the home they designed. This beautiful room features two stunning crystal chandeliers, several fine oil paintings and, from the windows, a glimpse of the veranda that stretches across the back of the house. Six tall white pillars guard this Southern-style "back porch." It overlooks a lawn sloping down to a wide stream.

When they can plan their vacations together, the Colemans travel. Sometimes, they "baby-sit." In 1976, they used three weeks of a month's holiday to stay with their grandchildren in sweltering Miami, while the parents took a badly needed vacation. The Justice confesses that she loves to cook and has always enjoyed domestic chores, except for sewing—an area in which she pleads lack of skill.

In spite of her early resolve to study law, and the rigors of her years of working her way through law school, Mary Coleman says she fully expected to stay at home while her children were very young. "Before they went to school," she says, "I felt it was important for me to be there." She says that she is very glad that she did not have to work full time then, but she is also happy that she was able to practice part-time many of those years. Was she worried, during this gap, that her career would wilt? "Not really," she says, "I just knew that I would get back to the law in some way." The astonishing success of her reentry should give heart to women everywhere whose views of the maternal role parallel those of Justice Coleman.

RUTH BADER GINSBURG

Women's Rights Advocate; Professor;
Counsel, American Civil Liberties Union

Ruth Bader Ginsburg is a serious person. She speaks slowly. The words are precise, selected with care. In every setting, the effort is appreciated. A casual visitor listens attentively and, on most occasions, is rewarded with a near-perfect understanding. In the formal, marbleized opulence of the U.S. Supreme Court building, it is no different. Hearing her argue the premier women's rights cases during the past decade, the Justices did not doze nor did they have doubt about her meaning. For Ruth Ginsburg, perhaps better than any lawyer in America, knows well and can map exactly the directions the law should take if the goal of equal rights for women is to be achieved.

Over the years, most students in her classes—at Rutgers or Harvard or Columbia—have followed with ease as she led them to and around the complex corners of the law. Those enrolled in procedure, conflict of laws, and federal courts courses, and, more recently, in sex-based discrimination seminars have been grateful for her lucid explanations. The same is true of thousands of additional law students throughout the country who use her books in comparative law and sex-based discrimination studies.

At home, the more ordinary messages to her son, her daughter, and her husband have been no less clear. Ruth Bader Ginsburg is a superb communicator—whether in a courtroom, classroom, or kitchen.

As the first Coordinator of the Women's Rights Project of the American Civil Liberties Union (ACLU), Ruth Ginsburg made a contribution to the developing law that was unique, and truly outstanding. The Project, which was the result of an ACLU decision to make gender equality in the law a priority effort, was launched following the landmark decision of the U.S. Supreme Court in the *Reed* case in 1971. In that case, the Court held invalid an Idaho statute that granted (under some circumstances) a preference to males as administrators of estates. It was the first time the Court had found a state statute to be in violation of the "equal protection" clause of the Fourteenth Amendment to the U.S. Constitution because of discrimination on the basis of sex. The *Reed* opinion was a call to arms. Troops were assembled and a strategy for attack was painstakingly planned. On several occasions in the years immediately following, the diminutive "General" Ginsburg stood before the Court to plead the cause.

She talks now about those crucial arguments, earnestly relating the details to the visitor in her austere office in the Columbia Law School complex. The office seems far removed from the Washington legal arena. It is clearly a working room, identical to the small, book-lined rectangles re-

served for law professors the country over—at one narrow
end, a door; at the other, a window with a view of a
dormitory.

How did it feel that first time she stood before the U.S.
Supreme Court? "I was terribly nervous," she says. "In fact,
I didn't eat lunch for fear that I might throw up." It is a
surprising confession from the self-assured woman who displays such a resolute calm. "Two minutes into my argument,
the fear dissolved," she continues. "Suddenly, I realized that
here before me were the nine leading jurists of America, a
captive audience. I felt a surge of power that carried me
through." That first time, it was the *Frontiero* case. It involved a female U.S. Air Force officer and the eligibility of
her husband for service-related benefits. Ms. Ginsburg and
Joe Levin of the Southern Poverty Law Center shared the
argument in the case, and they were successful in persuading the Court to rule in their favor. The Court decided that
the procedures for granting benefits to husbands, which
differed radically from those for Air Force wives, were in-
deed discriminatory.

Not long after this, Ruth Ginsburg was before the Court
again in the *Kahn* case. In that case, a widower challenged
the constitutionality of a Florida statute granting a small tax
exemption to widows. The result was different this time.
The Court upheld the law on the ground that it was reasonable for the state of Florida to grant special benefits to widows
as economically disadvantaged persons. The *Kahn* decision was a shock on two counts. It was an unexpected opinion, from an unexpected quarter. The author of it, former
Justice William O. Douglas, had been counted as a friend
by the women's rights advocates. "I was truly surprised,"
relates Ms. Ginsburg, "because Justice Douglas left the
bench about ten minutes into my argument and did not re-

turn. I took this as a signal that he had read the briefs and already leaned in our favor." Ms. Ginsburg confesses that, sometime later, when she read Douglas' book *Go East*, she understood. "In the book," she says, "he tells of the struggles his mother had after his father died . . . an event that occurred when Douglas was five years old."

The *Kahn* setback was small. In succeeding years, Ruth Ginsburg was back in Washington, winning landmark victories in Supreme Court cases involving the exclusion of women from Louisiana juries and the denial of certain social security benefits to widowers. The plaintiff in the *Weisenfeld* case was the young widower of a New Jersey school teacher who had been left, on her death, with the care of an infant. The case was special to Ruth Ginsburg. She had been with it all the way. It was she who made the initial argument before the three-judge federal District Court in New Jersey. The win in the Supreme Court was particularly satisfying.

In October 1976, Ms. Ginsburg stood before the Court to argue yet another social security case. Plaintiff Goldfarb, a widower not covered by social security, was denied benefits accrued by his deceased, wage-earning spouse because of a provision that he would be eligible for certain benefits only if his wife had contributed more than half of the funds for family support. In 1977, the Court held that this law was also discriminatory because it prescribed differing standards for eligibility.

Much of Ruth Ginsburg's in-depth knowledge of the baffling details of social security law had been gained years earlier. As the young bride of U.S. Army officer, Martin Ginsburg, who was stationed at Ft. Sill, Oklahoma, in the waning days of the Korean War, she had worked in a local social security office.

"I learned a great deal about the system," she recalls, "and as it happened, I also experienced discrimination there myself." She was originally hired as a GS-5 employee. But when she confided that she was pregnant, it was decided that she could not be sent to Baltimore for training, and she was given a GS-2 position instead. Though it paid much less, she recalls that she accepted the GS-2 assignment without complaint.

Ruth gave birth to her oldest child, Jane, in Oklahoma. That year, her genial husband Martin, who is now a successful tax lawyer in New York, completed his tour of duty. It was the only year of their married life that the energetic Ruth was not employed or in school. Not surprisingly, she tucked a correspondence course in accounting into this niche of free time. Years later, Martin would laughingly recall that, at this time, during Jane's infancy, a precedent was established that was often followed in the Ginsburg household in the years afterwards. It became Martin's chore to get up at night to answer calls from the nursery because he was "able to fall back to sleep more easily."

The next year found the Ginsburgs in Cambridge, Massachusetts. Both Martin and Ruth were busy at Harvard Law School—he in his second year, she as a freshman. It was a difficult time. They found an excellent baby-sitter to be with Jane during the days, but in the evenings they had to work out an intricate schedule so that each of them could get to the library for the necessary hours. "I found the first year of law school very hard," Ruth says. "I was much troubled by not having any sense of how I was doing." At Harvard, as at most law schools then and now, there were no examinations in most courses until the end of the year.

Incredibly, Ruth Ginsburg confesses that she might have dropped out if it had not been for her husband. Today, she candidly tells young girls considering the combination of career and family that a supportive husband is a "must." Asked if she could have achieved what she has without the helpful Martin, she says "no" with gusto. She adds, "What Martin did went far beyond support. He believed in me more than I believed in myself. All during that first year at Harvard when I was so concerned, he would tell people, 'my wife is going to make the Law Review.'"

Martin was right. Ruth did make top grades and the coveted *Law Review* slot. (Martin, though an excellent student, did not.) The next year, Martin was graduated. He located a position in New York and Ruth transferred to Columbia to complete law school. A year later, four-year-old Jane enlivened the graduation ceremonies at Columbia. Relatives still recount the tale. A startled Ruth, walking forward to pick up her diploma, heard a familiar voice sing out. "That's my Mommy," Jane told the hundreds of guests assembled in the hushed hall.

Ruth Ginsburg does not remember any particular event that set her on the path that led to that law diploma. The resolve did not come "like a thunderbolt." She cannot identify a moment of decision, but she can name a *person* who played a key role in it. Celia Ginsburg died when her daughter Ruth was only seventeen years old, but Ruth counts her influence as preeminent. "She was not a career woman," says Ruth. "She never worked outside the home, but she had a tremendous intellect." Ruth mourns the waste of talent, the fact that her mother was born in the wrong era.

Ruth Ginsburg does not recall that her mother urged her to study law, but she did impress upon young Ruth the idea that she should be independent, that she should develop her own abilities to the fullest. "I think of her often when I am in challenging situations that compel a top performance.

When I argue before the U.S. Supreme Court," Ruth says, "I wear her earrings and her pin and I think how pleased she would be if she were there."

Ruth Ginsberg rates discipline as an essential ingredient in her success in managing a career-family life-style, and she credits her mother with instilling that discipline. An older sister died at an early age, so Ruth was raised as an only child. "My father would have spoiled me," she says, "but my mother did not permit that. She was very strong, in every way but physical."

Ruth enrolled as a freshman at Cornell University in Ithaca, New York, in the fall of 1950. Recipient of a New York State scholarship and some additional help from the university, she also worked at a number of part-time clerical jobs during her college years to earn extra money. The decision to study law came sometime during her undergraduate days at Cornell. She recalls discussing it with her father. He had reservations. He did not object to her having a career, but he was concerned about her choosing to be a lawyer. Would she be able to make enough money to support herself? He worried because he had little to leave her.

At Cornell, Ruth Ginsburg spent much of her time with two other men who were major influences in her life. One was Martin, a fellow student whom she married upon graduation in 1954. The other was Professor Robert E. Cushman of the Cornell faculty who was her advisor, friend, and mentor. Majoring in government, she also took Professor Cushman's courses in constitutional law and pursued independent studies under his tutelage.

Does she recommend government as an undergraduate major for pre-law study? Not necessarily. "I tell students they should study what interests them," she says. Her own daughter entered Harvard Law School in the fall of 1977 and prepared by taking a master's degree in Italian Renaissance Studies at the University of Chicago.

Professor Ginsburg does feel that the ability to write well is a tremendous asset to law students and lawyers. "I am not sure just when or where I learned to write," she says. But she does recall that Professor Cushman, in reviewing her papers, took special interest and often added comments that improved her writing. Ms. Ginsburg is vocal in emphasizing the importance of developing good writing skills during pre-law days. She says, "The greatest failing among lawyers and law students is that many of them cannot write.. There is no question about it. It is true everywhere. In all the schools where I have taught, the examination papers bare the same problem. It is true of young lawyers and older lawyers. It is true of most of the briefs that I see."

She reaches across her desk to pick up a brief that she is reviewing. "This," she says, "is an exception. It is beautifully done . . . and rare." Although it was written by opposing counsel in a U.S. Supreme Court case that she is very interested in winning, she can say this. Secure, she can spare the praise. Scholarly in approach, Ruth Ginsburg bestows the admiring appraisal with ease. It is part of the principled style she exudes.

Her appearance fits the image. The brown hair is straight, pulled back taut against the sides of her head, securely bound by a ribbon at the back. It is a youthful profile—a balance to the tight set of the mouth and the serious eyes in the dark-tan face that has a just-back-from-Florida look at all times. There are few quick flashes of smile, no reassuring nods, no obligatory chuckles. The visitor feels a tension that seems to flow, not from any hint of nerves, but from the quietness of her manner . . . the tension perhaps of a brain ticking . . . searching ceaselessly for the citation, the phrase . . . weighing the moments for response, for action . . . the plan for the project, the book to come.

A superior student, Ms. Ginsburg did not anticipate any problem in finding a job after graduation from law school. Her services on the *Law Reviews* at both Harvard and Columbia seemed to guarantee the result. In fact, during her second year of law school, she recalls that she had no trouble in securing a summer position with one of the top law firms in New York. At work that summer, she applied herself with customary zeal.

"I thought I had done a terrific job," she says, "and I expected them to offer me a job on graduation." She was mistaken. No offer was forthcoming from that firm or, as it developed, from any other New York law firm. "At Columbia," she recalls, "I was interviewed by a dozen firms. Only two asked me for follow-up interviews at their offices. And I didn't get an offer from either of them."

The year was 1959 . . . mother in the *kitchen* was "crown princess." In the photographs on the "women's pages" of the daily newspapers, women carried babies, not briefcases. In the ladies' magazines, women were shown writing shopping lists, not briefs. In retrospect, Ruth Ginsburg feels certain that this climate had everything to do with her failure to secure a job with a law firm at that time.

The Ginsburg household was, of course, unusual for those days. Both Mom and Dad wrote briefs, and both shopped. "Whoever got home first cooked dinner," says Ruth. There was paid help, but household chores were shared too.

Very early, Martin began building an extensive tax library at home so that he could work there as well as at the office. (For some years now, his office has been a twenty-minute walk away.) Today, the west wall of the Ginsburg dining room contains Martin's equipment for dictating and is lined floor to ceiling, with books—law books to the left, a prize collection of cookbooks to the right. Martin Ginsburg is a pro in both the tax and culinary fields.

Jane is very close to both parents, but she says her conversations with them may be atypical. During a recent Sunday telephone call, she chatted with her mother about one of her classes and asked her Dad for a recipe. "On my next visit home," she says, "I might ask Dad if he will make chicken curry, if he has time."

Ruth Ginsburg says that finding help to care for Jane, and later for James, who was born in 1965, had not always been easy. She did not use day-care outside the home often nor did she call upon relatives frequently. Jane recalls that at a fairly early age she learned to get herself off to school in the mornings. For some periods, there was a live-in housekeeper with the Ginsburgs. At other times, help came in during the day.

There were moments of crisis. At age two and a half, James explored a cupboard under the kitchen sink and drank Drano. The horrified housekeeper wrapped him in a blanket and took a cab to the hospital. Minutes later, a terse message reached Ruth in the classroom and Martin at his office: "James drank Drano. Taken to nearest hospital." Both rushed, mistakenly, to the New York Medical Center. There was no record of their son's admittance. It was almost an hour later that word reached them that James was at the Lenox Hill Hospital. The confusion and delay were agonizing, but the worst moment was to come.

"When we first saw James," says Ruth, "we were stunned. Deep burns distorted his face, charred lips encircled his mouth—a tiny, burnt-out cavern, ravaged by the lye." The following days were a torment as doctors worked over the vital tissues. "Within a rather short time," says Ruth, "we knew that he would survive. But it was months before we knew whether the surgeons could restructure his horribly scarred features." Today, James is a lively soccer player with neat blond hair atop a bright round face that bears only the tiniest reminders of his tragic trip to the cupboard.

How did Ruth feel during this prolonged ordeal? As a working mother, did she agonize with regret that she had not been there when it happened? The answer is a qualified "yes." There were, she recalls, certainly feelings of guilt, tremendous guilt. On reflection, though, she says that perhaps the greater share of the guilt stemmed from horror at the awful error made in not putting the Drano out of the toddler's reach. She believes that the housekeeper, who rushed James to the hospital, did exactly the right thing.

It is a part of Ruth Ginsburg's success that she can view the incident in a relatively objective way. This attitude was helpful to her too during trying days with Jane who was, as a child, somewhat difficult at times. During her school days at the private girls' school, Brearley in New York, Jane had a record that she describes as "mixed."

During her senior year, she and a group of friends organized a memorable program called "A Symposium on Choices for Women," to which they attracted some of the leading career women in New York as speakers. There were other successes during her last years at Brearley, but the picture Jane paints of her earlier years there is quite different. "I didn't have many friends," she remembers, "and my behavior was very bad." Ruth and Martin went together to school conferences. Jane recalls that they were nearly always unhappy about the comments made about Jane's conduct. They were often upset by her behavior at home too. Violating strict rules, she recalls, she often bought candy after school, ate it and then lied about it. Was she punished? The answer is an emphatic "yes." "My parents were not permissive," says Jane. She feels too that they were united in their views, although her father was largely responsible for discipline in the Ginsburg household. She recalls that dinner conversation at the Ginsburgs was nearly always about law. "But if I had misbehaved, that would be the topic for the meal," she says.

Did Jane mind the fact that her mother worked? That she often had to baby-sit with her brother? Jane replies "no" to all such questions. She recalls that, over her school years, Brearley became less socialite-oriented and began to attract more children of professionals. During her elementary days, she recalls that she was sometimes the only one in the class whose mother worked. Much, much later, she says, a classmate of that period told her that she had often been pressed to bring Jane home for lunch by her own mother who "felt sorry" for Jane. Jane herself does not recall feelings of self-pity or resentment. "I think I rather enjoyed my situation," she says. "Since I was alone so much, I had more freedom. I got away with a lot."

It appears that the resourceful Jane also turned the baby-sitting chores to her advantage. On Sunday mornings when her exhausted parents slept in, Jane baby-sat with James. She was delighted with the excuse to drop Sunday school sessions at the nearby temple. "I think," she says, "that I also used my chores as an excuse to get out of a lot of other things I didn't want to do."

Ruth Ginsburg remembers that sometimes when Jane was mad about something she would tell her mother that when she grew up she would stay at home like her grandmother Ginsburg. Jane doesn't recall this. She does remember that she preferred to go with her grandmother on the annual fall shopping expeditions. Why? "Mother would just buy items needed. With my grandmother, I always got a lot of extras."

As a college student, Jane was exemplary. She completed the work for a bachelor's degree in history from the University of Chicago in three years, and she also worked at the campus radio station and helped organize the University Feminists Organization (UFO).

Today, Jane is brimming with admiration for her mother. In 1976, she traveled to Washington to hear her mother argue the *Goldfarb* case in the U.S. Supreme Court. She is close to her mother's work. "My 'professional association' with my mother began at a very early age," laughs Jane. The "association" has run the gamut over the years—from dull proofreading chores to exciting trips abroad, with visits to office and courtroom in between. Jane's first memory of such a visit is when Ruth was associated with the International Procedure Project in the early 1960s. Ruth had been lured to take part in this venture by the Director, Professor Hans Smit of the Columbia Law School. In accepting his offer, she paid a heavy price, for she had to reject a very attractive opportunity for employment with a major New York law firm.

"My luck in finding a position with a firm changed drastically," Ms. Ginsburg explains, "after I had clerked for two years to Judge Edward Palmeri of the U.S. District Court for the Southern District of New York." Ruth got that job because of her fine academic performance, which placed her on the list of students Columbia Law School would recommend for clerkships. Since at the time of graduation the doors of New York firms had been firmly closed to Ruth, she was happy to take this position.

Ruth developed a warm relationship with Judge Palmeri and she regards those years as his clerk as a stimulating and valuable experience. Afterwards, there were many opportu-

nities for positions with firms. However, as a dedicated
scholar, Ruth Ginsburg decided that the work on the International Project had more appeal. As it developed, there was
ample challenge. The Project work was arduous. At its end,
Ruth Ginsburg emerged as author, with Anders Bruzelius,
of a two-volume text on Swedish procedural law. In be-
ween, there were two summers of research labor in Sweden
—one in Lund, the other in Stockholm.

Jane went along to Lund, and Martin joined them for
some weeks that summer. The second year, Jane lived in a
children's home, which was a kind of camp in the country,
some miles south of Stockholm. Once they were back in New
York, Jane remained close to the Project during the dreary
months when the books were in production. Taught to read
by her mother when she was very young, Jane vividly recalls
the long hours when she helped with proofreading of the
text.

In 1962, Ruth began what was to be a nine-year stint,
teaching at Rutgers University Law School in Newark, New
Jersey. Meeting her responsibilities across the Hudson River
during those years was far from easy. Ruth recalls that the
time of James' birth was an especially difficult one for the
Ginsburgs. James arrived, conveniently enough, in early
September, just before the fall term. But in the meantime,
Ruth's critically ill father had moved in with them. Ruth
and Martin had to do yeoman work in finding and scheduling
help and, often, filling in the gaps themselves. Somehow,
they managed to provide the unbroken hours of care that
were required for their infant son, lively daughter, and ailing
parent. Did Ruth ever consider taking leave then? The reply
is negative.

Commuting from New York City to Newark, as Ruth did
all those years, was a chore in itself. Furthermore, it took a

large chunk of time each day. Mostly, Ruth put the hours to good use. She recalls that she often used the time on the subway to read mail, saving the train time for final class preparation. Ruth Ginsburg's efficiency is pervasive, habitual. According to Martin, she often works in cabs on the way to the theater.

What are the diversions for the Ginsburgs? They enjoy music; they attend opera regularly. Some years ago, they joined a club north of the city. On pleasant weekends, they head up there for golf.

Ruth Ginsburg rates herself as energetic and admits that she has, on occasion, worked around the clock. Six hours is a good night's sleep. During the week, she often manages with three or four hours a night and then catches up with a ten hour stretch on a weekend. A "night person," she regularly retires in the early hours of the morning. James recalls that he got up very early one morning, about 5 A.M., and discovered his mother still at work at the dining room table. The table was littered with books and papers and an open box of prunes—a favorite snack. "I guess I work this way," she admits, "because I am so fussy about the quality of the product."

In 1970, Ruth Ginsburg was a Visiting Professor at the Harvard Law School. Since the fall term of 1971, she has served as Professor at Columbia University Law School. In a recent semester at Columbia, she taught constitutional law and the sex-discrimination course. The text for the latter was *Cases and Materials on Sex-Based Discrimination,* a book that she wrote together with Herma Kay and Kenneth Davidson. During the time that the text was in production, she used many of the materials in mimeograph form in her classes.

Ruth Ginsburg has somehow found time to fulfill varied

and vital positions in professional groups over the years. She has served as a member of key committees of the American Bar Association (ABA) and the Association of American Law Schools (AALS). Deeply interested in the women's role, she served as presiding member of the AALS committee on women in legal education in 1972. At that time, she coordinated a symposium on the law school curriculum and the legal rights of women. Since 1973, she has been a member of the Board of Editors of the ABA *Journal,* a publication mailed monthly to more than two hundred thousand lawyers who are members of this influential organization. In May of 1978, she was elected to the Council of the American Law Institute.

Since joining the staff at Columbia Law School, she has been on a reduced teaching schedule that varies according to her duties at the ACLU. She is still counsel to the Women's Rights Project and works closely with the present Coordinator, Kathleen Perratis, an attractive University of Southern California law graduate who came to the ACLU from a Los Angeles law firm. Ms. Perratis is lavish in praising Ruth Ginsburg, giving her high marks for judgment, writing skill, and research standards. "She is," says Ms. Perratis, "just the most spectacular lawyer I have ever met." She describes Ms. Ginsburg as very exacting, but says that even when she is critical, she is very fair. "Always," says Ms. Perratis, she is most appreciative of superior effort.

Ruth Ginsburg says that she probably works a minimum of twelve hours a day. She estimates that about half of her time is devoted to ACLU concerns. She is on the National Board and also serves as one of the four General Counsels of the organization. She journeys regularly from her 118th Street office at Columbia down to the national headquarters on East 40th Street for meetings of the ACLU legal staff. The

ACLU offices on the tenth floor of the drab midtown building are spartan, the furnishings functional. The emphasis is
on output, on the mapping of actions that will make a difference. It is a setting that matches the aims of Ruth Ginsburg.
The ACLU owes much to this slim woman who moves quietly through its rooms, keeping its massive legal engine
tuned to respond to the most significant legal issues of the
times.

CARLA ANDERSON HILLS

*Former Cabinet Member; Practicing
Lawyer; Administrator; Author*

When Carla Hills was sworn in by President Ford as Secretary of the U.S. Department of Housing and Urban Development (HUD) in March 1975, she became a member of the President's cabinet. In doing so, she joined a very small group of United States citizens who have been privileged to function as the nation's top advisors, and an even more exclusive category of American women. In the two-hundred-year history of the nation, only two women before her had served in the cabinet as heads of major government agencies. They were Frances Perkins of the U.S. Department of Labor, who was appointed by President Franklin Roosevelt, and Oveta Culp Hobby of the Department of Health, Education and Welfare, who served in the Eisenhower administration.)

The appointment brought headlines. Reading the news, friends and former colleagues of Carla Hills were pleased. It is doubtful that many of her acquaintances were very surprised. Those who had known her at Stanford University, where she received her undergraduate degree, or at Yale Law School, from which she was graduated in 1958, would remember her as a top student.

Colleagues from her days in the U.S. Attorney's office and her years of private practice in Los Angeles would remember her as an outstanding lawyer both in the courtroom and in the offices of the law firm of Munger, Tolles, Hills & Rickerhauser where she was a partner. Lawyers and law students concerned with antitrust and federal practice matters had, for years, known and respected Carla Hills as an authority whose books and lectures brought welcome guidance.

To the scores of attorneys who had been serving under Mrs. Hills' leadership in the Civil Division of the U.S. Department of Justice since April 1974, the news brought mixed feelings. There was enthusiasm for her success, mingled with genuine regret that she would be moving across the Mall, leaving the old gray building on Constitution Avenue for the new gray building on Seventh Street in Southwest Washington.

Women friends and fellow mothers who knew Carla Hills' four young children and had watched their growth and nurture had long regarded her as a "superwoman." But the person who was perhaps the least surprised by the appointment was her husband and chief cheerleader, Roderick Hills. A brilliant lawyer, his own career had been, like Carla's, studded with honors. Since graduation from law school, both have moved straight up the ladder in the legal profession.

They met when he was at Stanford Law School, where he edited the *Law Review* and was a member of the Order of the Coif. The courtship continued on the East Coast when he was clerk of the late Justice Stanley Reed of the U.S. Supreme Court and she was at Yale. Marriage followed shortly after her graduation. During the next three years, Carla served in the office of the U.S. District Attorney for the Southern District of California and Roderick practiced with a Los Angeles firm. In 1962, he organized the firm in which he and Carla were partners for so many years. During the Ford administration, he served as Counsel to the President and later as Chairman of the powerful U.S. Securities & Exchange Commission.

Among those who did not cheer Carla Hills' appointment to HUD were Senator William Proxmire and a few others on Capitol Hill. They grumbled at her confirmation hearings that she had no expertise in housing matters. What they did not then know, but later came to appreciate, was that Carla Hills happened to be a lawyer with an amazing aptitude for administration.

The penthouse suite of offices from which Carla Hills directed operations as Secretary of HUD is impressive. A visitor who had an appointment with her moved through a secretarial maze separating the hallway from her huge office to the left of the interior reception room. Many who came to attend meetings were steered to the right, into the enormous conference room, where they sat in high-backed leather chairs flanking a massive oval table.

If lunch was planned, they moved to assemble around a table only slightly smaller in the adjacent dining room where tasteful paintings and a silver tea service complimented the elegant decor. In each of the rooms, huge windows afforded visitors a panoramic view of the Potomac River.

The Potomac's course from Washington to the Atlantic is southeasterly and relatively short. By contrast, the directives of HUD spin out to every corner of the nation and across thousands of miles. The regional offices of HUD function as nerve centers, relaying messages both to and from

Washington—sometimes, but not always, absorbing the attendant shocks. The task of implementing the complex federal housing laws that falls to HUD is enormous. Sharp critical reactions are an almost unavoidable part of the game. A single decision in Washington often affects thousands of citizens, and hundreds of contractors, bankers, and union laborers throughout the country.

Assisting Secretary Hills in running this vast and volatile enterprise were four Special Assistants, the Regional Directors, and a departmental staff numbering in the thousands nationwide. Within a relatively short time, there were few in the house of HUD who did not know Carla Hills was in full command. She approached her new duties with a mind open to receive information, but firmly fixed on the way she would operate in meeting agency mandates.

Her first rule, which she has always applied in dealing with staff at the office or in the home, is that she does not expect anyone to do anything that she wouldn't do herself. The prescription is hardly original. What may be new, and what has inspired the deep respect of staff members, is that Carla Hills follows the rule scrupulously. She admits too that an important corollary to the rule is that, "There are not many things I am unwilling to do." Three different staff members at HUD mentioned, in tones of visible awe, that Mrs. Hills often took the "red-eye" flights back from the West Coast. (Those are the late-evening flights which, with crossing of time zones, bring passengers to Washington, D.C., in the early hours of the following day, not long before sunrise and the morning rush hour.)

Asked if legal training is helpful in administration, Mrs. Hills hesitates. "Some lawyers are good administrators and some are bad. As a group, I don't think that lawyers are any better or worse than others." However, she feels that her particular legal background in the courtrooms of southern California was especially helpful. "Such work," she says, "trains you to identify the issues. Also, cross-examination skills are useful in getting the facts."

At HUD, getting the facts was a big job. Carla Hills' action plan was grounded upon a three-step analysis.

1) You can't have efficiency without accountability;
2) You can't have accountability without deadlines;
3) You can't have credibility without meeting deadlines.

Following these steps, Carla Hills set about improving the credibility of an agency widely lambasted by the public it served and the taxpayers who supplied its funds. She also had to deal with the restive legislators on the Hill who were stuck with the task of trying to keep both of these groups happy. She confesses that, initially, it was a challenge to determine the scope and lines of responsibility within the agency. Most staff members welcomed the setting of specific goals and deadlines. Most worked hard to meet them.

Throughout her tenure at HUD, one goal ranked high. Carla Hills fought hard to avoid waste and to conserve the available United States housing stock. In September 1975, she told the Women Lawyers Association of Los Angeles (a group she had once served as president): "One of my first priorities is the job of helping to preserve and recycle our cities. We must reverse the notion that blossomed in the last decade that the best way to cope with a worn-out neighborhood was to throw it away and build a new one farther out."

Carla Hills is a firm believer in the technique of "management by objectives." It was a part of her own life-style long before it became fashionable in the business world. "I am," says Carla Hills, "an inveterate list-maker." Goals at the office are specific. One such goal, which she established soon after assuming office, involved the disposition of vast numbers of properties repossessed by HUD on government mortgage defaults. Responsibilities were defined and targets established for each region. There were problems. At one point, a federal judge in Chicago threatened to jail her and Regional Director John Waner for failure to supply vast amounts of data requested in a related class action suit. She also faced an angry citizens group and a barrage of verbal assaults at a large meeting in the Windy City.

However, it was not long before measurable results began to come in. The staff was cheered by the progress made in meeting goals. Carla Hills had drawn upon her trial experience to map strategies. "In planning a trial," she says, "you draw a blueprint. Each witness, each piece of evidence, is a part of the mosaic. You work to develop a picture that will convince the trier of fact." In running an agency, she feels the administrator has much the same task—to build a convincing picture that will motivate staff. "Team effort is directly related to the clarity of the overall design," she says.

Carla Hills also believes that a good administrator must "get there earlier and stay later." During the years at HUD, she routinely worked from 7 A.M. to 7 P.M. and took home a batch of material to read each night. Debby Abbott, her "scheduler" at HUD, reported that the twelve-hour days were closely scheduled, with one exception. Mrs. Hills insisted that time be allowed between meetings to return phone calls, a task to which she assigned a high priority. Her schedule while on the road was always tighter, because she preferred to get the job done and get back to Washington. While she was at HUD, Saturdays were workdays and often, some time on Sunday had to be set aside for work too.

Beverly Posey, Mrs. Hills' long-time secretary, testifies that Carla Hills' work habits were not new ones. She recalls that in California Mrs. Hills had often dictated briefs from poolside while watching her children. Her dedication has inspired fierce devotion from those who work for her. When Carla Hills moved from Los Angeles to Washington, both housekeeper and secretary came along. In Mrs. Posey's case, it meant moving her own family, and a new job for her husband. Mrs. Hills says that, for this reason, she tried to talk her out of the move. But she readily admits that she was delighted to have her talented co-worker with her for the challenging work at HUD.

No one says that Carla Hills is "easy" to work for. She is exacting in her expectations, and it is a part of her style to let the staff know when she is unhappy with results. However, associates testify that she is extremely fair in her judgments, and she has a reputation for thoughtfulness. James Walker, her administrative aide at HUD, remembers her personal call to him at the time his father died. Many staff members recall with pleasure the parties she arranged for them to have on the presidential yacht, *Sequoia*.

When she came to HUD, Carla Hills said, "I would like to be remembered not as the best *woman* Secretary, but as the best Secretary HUD ever had." There is plenty of evidence that she took giant steps toward achieving that goal during her tenure at HUD, which was just short of two years. At the time she left HUD, many staff members wrote personal letters to her confiding their admiration for the job she had done there. And on Capitol Hill, Thomas L. Ashley, an Ohio Congressman with a special interest in housing, confessed that his initial skepticism had long been replaced by a keen respect for Carla Hills' abilities.

A similar attitude prevails among the attorneys she

worked with at the Department of Justice. An attorney in the Patent Litigation Division of the Civil Division was one of a group of lawyers who met with her in connection with a very complicated patent case. "She had had little briefing," he said "and I was astonished at the speed with which she picked up the issues." "Brilliant!"—the word he chooses— is a word commonly used by those who try to describe Carla Hills.

Husband Roderick calls her "bright, organized, and cheerful." His obvious respect for Carla's legal talent has gone a lot further than verbal tributes. Not every husband would encourage his wife to assume partnership with several other lawyers in a newly organized firm. Not every husband would recommend his wife for a high-level government position thousands of miles away, as he is said to have done.

As a Republican active in the campaign of Senator Kuchel of California, Roderick came to know Elliot Richardson, then Secretary of Defense and later U.S. Attorney General. It was reported that he tried to persuade Roderick to take a government post, but, in the fall of 1973, he offered Carla the opportunity to head the Civil Division of the Department of Justice. It is a key position, sometimes described as a kind of proving ground for federal judicial candidates. Chief Justice Burger of the U.S. Supreme Court is among the many prominent figures who have served in this post.

It was a tempting offer and Carla decided to accept it. On the day she located a house for the family in the Washington area, she flew back to the West Coast. The date was October 20, the Saturday of the famous "Saturday night massacre." While Mrs. Hills was airborne, Richardson resigned. Nonetheless, the wheels, although slowed, moved forward. In April 1974, she began work at the Department of Justice.

Just eleven months later, she became Secretary of HUD and a member of President Ford's cabinet. In the fall of 1975, Justice Douglas resigned from the U.S. Supreme Court. Carla Hills' name was among those most often mentioned as probable appointees to the seat on the highest Court. The seat eventually was occupied by Justice John Paul Stevens.

Not long after Carla began her work at the U.S. Department of Justice, Roderick was appointed a counsel to the President. The Hills settled in. Housekeeper Nellie Spolders took charge at the house and the Hills children looked over their new schools. Although family roots run deep in the California soil, it was not the first time the Hills had moved their brood. The 1969–70 school term found the family in Cambridge, Massachusetts, where Roderick was a Visiting Professor at the Harvard Law School, and Carla wrote a book titled, *The Anti-Trust Advisor.*

At the time of the move to Washington, Laurie Hills was twelve, Roderick Jr. (Ricky) was nine, Megan, eight, and Allison (Lisa) was three. With both parents working long hours, family life for the Hills children was, in some respects, unique. Saturdays, for example, often meant trips to Dad's office in the White House. Sometimes, the kids took homework along or books to read. On quieter days, they were permitted to do a bit of exploring.

Carla gives high marks to Rod for his willingness to help with family responsibilities. Asked if a woman could build a top legal career and raise a family without a supportive spouse, Carla Hills says, "I don't see how you could do it if you had to go home every night and fight over who would do the household chores."

For his part, Rod says he is "no paragon." But he admits that he pitches in when help is needed. He stresses that the children are expected to help too. "Last fall," he says, "Laurie had the job of raking the leaves. She subcontracted some of the work to the other children, but the job got done."

A prodigious worker himself, Rod recalls that he had his first job at age ten, weeding in a nursery near his California home. As a teenager, he had a thriving business as a door-to-door citrus salesman, marketing the fruits of the orange trees in the Hills' yard. A good shopper, he frequently buys the groceries and clothes for the children. A conscientious father, he has spent many hours with Ricky's Indian Guide groups. Each August, he and Ricky head for the Hills' shack in Idaho for a fishing vacation with another father-son duo who are good friends. There have been interesting trips for the whole family too, including, in the summer of 1977, a six-week trek through Europe.

All of the Hills children are interested in music. Neither parent claims credit for their talents, but Rod does admit that he played in a jazz band in college. Megan, an admirer of Dorothy Hamill, is a fine ice skater. Her athletic talent may be inherited from Carla, who is an excellent tennis player and was captain of the women's tennis team at Stanford. Although interests have shifted from time to time, the Hills children have always been involved in a variety of activities. Nellie is often at the wheel, as car pools are a more or less permanent part of the daily routine.

During the years when both Rod and Carla were working twelve and fourteen-hour days, Nellie was a mainstay. Carla Hills says that finding persons like Nellie is, without question, one of the most difficult aspects of the combining of a career with family life. She feels she has been fortunate. Nellie has been with the Hills since 1969 and, over the years, there have been only three housekeepers.

Carla Hills has a talent for selection and for building solid relationships. Can she offer any tips? She says she approaches the task of interviewing a housekeeper with the same gravity that she would approach selection of a key member of her professional staff. She feels that there should be little compromise on standards but, she cautions, "you have to be willing to pay what is needed to attract persons of the highest caliber." Although the Hills' housekeepers have been extraordinary, Mrs. Hills mentions another important element in the success story. "We have had excellent health," she says, "and that is vital. I would have quit in a minute if any serious problems developed."

Carla Hills admits that there are some tasks that just can't be delegated. Over the years, she has worked out a well-defined approach to parent responsibilities related to the children's schools. She gives little time to attending parent meetings, but she has always contributed to school enrichment activities, often arranging special trips to the courtroom for class groups. She also gives top priority to attending all programs in which the children are participating. She believes, "There is a time when *presence* is all-important." She counts appearances at such events as more significant than merely being there for a quick "hello-good-bye" when the children come home from school and rush out to play with friends.

Mrs. Hills says that she has always gone to great lengths to be sure she can mesh school events into her busy schedule. Often, she calls the school principal at the beginning of each term and asks the dates when programs are scheduled so that they can go on her calendar at the earliest opportunity. "I make a major effort to arrange travel so that I can be there. Sometimes, if all else fails, I go to a rehearsal," she says. This might be necessary, she notes, if she has a corporate board meeting on the West Coast on the same day as one of Ricky's recitals. (In 1977, she was on the Boards of four major U.S. corporations—International Business Machines (IBM), Southern California Edison, Standard Oil Company of California, and The Signal Companies, Inc.) On some occasions, she has made changes in her professional commitments to attend school events. Does she tell other lawyers or aides the reason? "Now, I often do," she says. But she confesses that, in the early days, she seldom explained why she was requesting a change in plans. It is a telling comment, reflecting the security of her position in today's legal world.

In the spring of 1977, when Megan was in the school production of "The Wizard of Oz," Carla wrote a note on Megan's script reminding her to find out the times of the performances. Notes are a pervasive part of the Hills household —reminders on the bulletin board, messages in lunch boxes. Often, there are notes *to* Carla from the children—sometimes on her pillow so she will see them when she comes in late at night.

During the busy years, there were long naps in the afternoon for the younger children so that they could stay up for dinner with their parents at 8 P.M. or later. Carla Hills feels that this flexibility is another of the key ingredients in the success of a family-career combination. She notes that in the Anderson household when she was a child, her mother always served dinner at 6 P.M., and hours for the day's activities were more or less fixed.

Carla describes her own childhood in the suburbs of Los Angeles as "advantaged." But she is quick to add that references to her family's wealth have been "overblown." She offers an example. "The home we moved to when I was fifteen years old was very nice, but it was *not* used as the set for the movie *Sunset Boulevard* as has been reported. It was one of several homes panned by the cameras during a street view." She says the family had happy times at the place they owned in Burbank, but the "estate" was only about ten acres. "We did have horses," she laughs, "but we also had an ordinary vegetable garden." She recalls that although her mother had some help, she did cook and perform other domestic tasks common to most middle-class homemakers. "My brother and I weren't raised by a staff of servants," she says.

At about age ten, Carla Anderson decided to become a lawyer. Why? She isn't sure, but she says that lawyer Alexander Hamilton was one of her heroes. She was an avid reader, with a special interest in history.

Over the years, her resolve to study law stuck, in the face of much discouraging advice. She recalls discussing her plans with a teacher during her junior year of high school. The teacher tried to talk her out of attending law school, commenting that it would be a waste because she "would just get married and have a family." Her advisor at Stanford objected too, but on different grounds. He did not feel it was the best course of study for her. Both responses were surprising in light of the circumstances in which they were made. The private high school she attended was not a fashionable finishing school, but rather an academically-oriented institution that sent nearly every graduate on to college. At Stanford, Carla's record was scarcely one to foster doubts about her aptitude for law studies. Her junior year was spent in study at Oxford in England and she was graduated the following year *cum laude* from Stanford.

At home, she faced stronger opposition. Her mother worried about whether a career would cause her to delay, or perhaps miss, marriage and a family. Her father had other doubts. He was a transplanted Missourian who had worked hard to build a prospering building materials business in southern California. The business was everything to him. Reflecting on his attitude toward her plan to study law, Carla says, "I think he found it almost inconceivable that I might find a career outside the business more enjoyable. I am sure that he did not mind me having a career, but he was most anxious that I join the business. He would have liked me to handle the financial end of it." She also comments, "Nor was it a question of his treating me as a son. My brother, Stephen (who now runs the business), and I were treated with total equality."

Carl Anderson had another objection. He did not want his daughter to go East to school. When the time came to choose a college, Carla had wanted to attend Radcliffe, but her father insisted that she choose between Stanford and the University of Southern California. The battle was joined again when she was admitted to Yale Law School in New Haven, Connecticut, but Carla was determined to go—with or without his approval. Over time, Carl Anderson's position softened and he became very proud of his lawyer daughter. "I think," says Carla, "that, at first, he was afraid I would go East and marry and stay there, and he couldn't bear the thought of my being so remote from California."

At Stanford, Carla Anderson worked on the school newspaper in spare moments. Her majors were in history and economics. Did she feel at Yale Law School or in later years that this was good preparation for the law? "I don't think," she says, "that there is any demonstrable evidence to prove that any one pre-law course is better than another. It is important to learn to write well and to take courses that force you to use your mind fully." She does feel that a knowledge of economics is most useful because so many decisions hinge on economic factors.

At Yale, she was graduated in 1958 in a class of one hundred and eighty students, of which five were women. She says that she has been lucky in the matter of sex discrimination, that she has not been refused employment on account of sex. But she also admits that she had limited experience in the job *seeking* arena. She has joined women's groups, but is not a militant feminist. She states quite frankly that she does not get excited over details such as whether mail is addressed to her as Mrs., Ms., or, as is sometimes the case, Mr.

Some of her colleagues say that they think of her as a man. She is not insulted. She takes the comment, as she believes it is meant, as a tribute to her legal skills and to her ability to neutralize the sex factor in professional relationships.

What advice will she offer her own daughters? The reply is indirect. She firmly believes that everyone should "go the distance that they can go"—working to their fullest potential. She feels that many women make the mistake of underestimating their capabilities. "It saddens me," she says, "to see so many women not using their talents."

She says that she always planned to have a career *and* a family. Over the years, has the task of combining career and family been easier, or more difficult than she expected? She says only that it has been "terrific."

What advice does she give to young women who contemplate taking this road? "I don't tell them it will be easy," she says, "but I guess I suggest that, if one is determined, there is a way to work things out." She readily concedes that good health and a supportive spouse have been vital elements in whatever success she has achieved. Nor does she discount the importance of organizational expertise on both the professional and personal levels. The lists she makes *do* organize her goals; ingenuity and energy help her to fit them into a workable daily round. Sometimes, it means skipping lunch. Often, it means washing her hair late at night because a stop at the hairdresser will subtract precious hours from a busy morning.

Generous in the plaudits she gives her own husband for his willingness to help at home, she sees cultural biases concerning the stereotyped assignment of household tasks fading somewhat. Has resentment against the working mother vanished? Will it in the near future? She isn't sure. She admits to having felt the sting of criticism. "I've had my share of unpleasant comments like, 'Don't you hate not having time for your children?', but I have developed a tough skin concerning personal assaults."

Since 1978 a senior resident partner in the Washington, D.C. office of the firm of Latham, Watkins & Hills, Carla Hills has performed with distinction a series of fascinating assignments. As a practicing lawyer, she made herself at home in both the courtroom and the law office. She has written about the law and administered some of the most complex laws on the federal statute books. She has taught law to students at U.C.L.A. Law School and lectured at Harvard and Yale Law Schools. Which of these tasks did she most enjoy? She refuses to choose a favorite. "I have lived my life in chapters," she says. "I have enjoyed them all . . . and I look forward to those that are yet to come."

JEWEL STRADFORD LaFONTANT

Former Deputy U.S. Solicitor General;
Corporate Director; Practicing Lawyer

"Women lawyers have a higher degree of credibility than other females," says Jewel LaFontant. "There is less of a burden on us to prove ourselves." People tend to think of legal training as tough and demanding, she says, and this helps to erase, in the public mind, the image of the dim or flighty female. The comment is consistent with Jewel La-Fontant's cheerful, confident outlook. It is a positive world view that has been with her throughout the three decades of her remarkable climb from legal aid lawyer for United Charities in Chicago to a post at the pinnacle of public advocacy in this country—that of Deputy Solicitor General of the United States.

When she was graduated in 1946 from the University of Chicago Law School, she became one of the few females who was then a part of the legal profession; as a black female attorney she was a member of an even tinier fraternity; as a Republican in Chicago, she was miles from the mainstream.

Today, seated across the gleaming glass table that rests on thick gold carpeting in her posh modern office overlooking the towering First National Bank building, she is a part of the Establishment, a comfortable, sought-after participant in the contemporary scene.

Beautifully dressed, at ease, and speaking in a magnetic, melodious voice, Jewel LaFontant greets the visitor cordially. Her gaze is direct. Her shoulders are straight and they are, the visitor soon learns, almost totally free of "chips." She recalls the "sit-ins" and the early days of her civil rights practice, but it is apparent that she has given little time to rancor. With Jewel LaFontant, the emphasis is on one-to-one relationships, on "making friends." She was an officer of the Chicago arm of the National Association for the Advancement of Colored People (NAACP); she was also a member, many years ago, of the Board of Managers of the largely white Chicago Bar Association. Today, she sits, with equal aplomb, on the boards of six major U.S. corporations—The Equitable Life Assurance Society of the U.S., Hanes Corporation, Transworld Airlines, Bendix Corporation, Foote, Cone & Belding, and Continental Bank of Chicago. A wife and mother and, during most of these years, an active practicing lawyer, Jewel LaFontant has made a leap matched by few individuals—men or women, black or white.

How did she do it? Listening to her talk about her perception of the problems, her acceptance of the realities, and her formula for mixing good will with a resolve to alter narrow views, the visitor begins to understand the magic.

Long active in the Republican Party, Jewel LaFontant was offered several positions in Washington when the party came to power in the late 1960s. She was reluctant to leave her Chicago practice, but she says that the opportunity to serve as Deputy Solicitor General of the United States,

which came in 1973, is the one offer that she could not refuse. "I accepted," she says, "because I am a lawyer first of
all, and I considered this to be one of the top legal assignments in the nation." The Solicitor General represents the
U.S. government when it is a party to cases that reach the
U.S. Supreme Court. As federal counsel, the Solicitor General must also decide on the actions to be taken, or not taken,
on behalf of the government in the hundreds of other court
decisions rendered annually that may be subject to review
by the high Court.

There are three Divisions in the Solicitor General's office—
Civil Rights, Criminal, and Civil. Each is headed by a Deputy who makes recommendations to the Solicitor General
regarding the course of action to be followed in Division
matters. As Deputy, Mrs. LaFontant was in charge of the
Civil Division, an office that handles a wide variety of cases.
Civil Division lawyers deal with tax questions, immigration
matters, and a miscellany of other issues.

As Deputy Solicitor for the Civil Division from 1973 to
1975, Jewel LaFontant participated, by her own count, in
the review of over five thousand cases. As a representative
of the Solicitor General, she argued seven cases in the U.S.
Supreme Court during this period. (She won six and lost
one, the latter a 5 to 4 decision.)

The first of the cases Jewel LaFontant argued in the Supreme Court was a tax case in which the opponent was the
State Tax Commission of Mississippi. There were a few problems. First off, there was little time for her to get ready.
Erwin Griswold, then Solicitor General, wasted no time in
putting Mrs. LaFontant to work. She had been in the office
only about ten days when he assigned this argument to her.
It was set for March 19. She worried because she had only
two weeks to prepare.

She also fretted about another, less important, concern. What would she wear? Earle Malkin, a partner in her Chicago law firm, had reminded her that the Solicitor General (or his male designate) always wore a morning suit— black cutaway jacket, dress shirt, and striped trousers. With the help of Malkin's wife, Bonnie, a talented designer and seamstress, Mrs. LaFontant electrified the Court when she appeared in a specially designed outfit that paralleled the traditional costume—a frilled white blouse with a black wool jacket and a gray pin-striped skirt. A tall, handsome woman with a striking figure, Jewel LaFontant confesses that she has always liked "pretty things." But she says that there has been precious little time for shopping or keeping abreast of fashions. She notes, with some delight, that in 1975 she was voted "Stylemaker of the Year" by the International Association of Cosmetologists. "I went to Atlantic City to get my award, just like Miss America," she says.

During the customary pre-argument chat in the Mississippi tax case, one of the opposing parties complained, in jest, that his lawyer wasn't as "pretty" as the United States government representative. Jewel LaFontant says that she has learned, over the years, to ignore that sort of sexist comment. But all the same, she was pleased, when at a luncheon months later, Justice Brennan of the U.S. Supreme Court remarked, "I want you to know, Mrs. LaFontant, that when you walk into the courtroom, the Justices always take note." She recalls that Chief Justice Burger has often been critical of the nongovernment lawyers who appear before the Court in baggy suits and garish ties. "I think," concludes Mrs. La-Fontant, "that the Justices appreciated my costume, not because of my particular appearance but because the special effort showed respect for the Court."

Jewel LaFontant had respect too for the heavy demands

of her new job. She recalls her first meeting with Griswold and his first words to her. "Young woman, if you think this will be an easy job, you are mistaken." Somewhat taken aback, she assured Griswold that she had always worked hard and planned to continue doing so. She might have added that she had spent far more hours in the courtroom than many of the well-known lawyers who are, with each change of administration, summoned to Washington on high-level legal assignments.

In the early days of her civil rights practice in Chicago, Jewel LaFontant was often in court. "Routinely," she says, "we would sit in and then sue." She appears in the local courtrooms less frequently now because she confines her practice largely to corporate and appellate matters. She represented the wife of Muhammad Ali in a recent divorce action, but she spends less time on matrimonial cases these days. Now, criminal cases are referred to a cousin, but for many years, she did a great deal of criminal work. "I thought it was very valuable," she says, "because it brought me to court more often." Civil matters, she notes, are most often settled without trial or any court exposure at all. She says her criminal practice never brought any problems, although she defended murderers and dealt with almost every sort of criminal. The only case she can recall turning down was a heinous multiple rape. "Women," she says, "can do any kind of legal work." She deplores the trend to shunt women lawyers into narrow fields, such as "affirmative action," for example. Too often, she feels, the women in the legal profession are steered away from the more lucrative areas of specialization.

She has high praise for court work and encourages young attorneys to seek this experience. She says, "Trial work helps you to move. Even if you don't stay in it, it gives you self-confidence you can't get elsewhere. Nothing is more satisfying than standing up in front of a judge and *selling* your position. "Selling," she says, "is what the law is all about."

Jewel LaFontant is a star salesman, and a cool one. She won the Mississippi tax case despite an emergency that brought her, most abruptly, before the Court to make the crucial argument. As it happened, a lawyer in the case scheduled just ahead of hers suffered a heart attack and was rushed to the hospital. "Can *you* begin now?" an aide asked. She nodded and stepped up to give a top performance. Two circumstances helped.

For one thing, her fourteen-year-old son John was sitting in the audience. Throughout her stay in Washington, she commuted to Chicago on weekends in order that John might continue his schooling at the Laboratory School of the University of Chicago. Many Fridays, she hurried to watch *his* performances there on the basketball court. Now, she was anxious that he see *her* at her best. She confesses that his comment afterwards was a bit of a letdown. Leaving the courtroom, she asked him, "How did I do?" She smiles at the reply. "Well, at least I could hear you, Mom. I couldn't hear the other lawyer," said the serious John.

There was another good reason for Jewel LaFontant to be confident in the marble hall of the high Court. It was not the first time she had argued there. As a private practitioner, she had brought a narcotics case to the U.S. Supreme Court some half-dozen years earlier. She had won that case too, persuading the Court to reverse a holding of the Supreme Court of Illinois. That case concerned the admissibility of a confession used in the trial in which the defendant was convicted, a very different issue. She notes another difference between the two cases. "I knew that case inside out; I had ived with it and worked on it for two years—not two weeks!" he says.

Had she been nervous that first time? "I was more excited han frightened," she says. What was she thinking of as she entered the courtroom? "I thought about my father," she ays, "who had appeared before the U.S. Supreme Court in he early 1940s." A student then at Oberlin College, Jewel had come to watch him. The case was *Hansberry* v. *Lee*, one of the first restrictive covenant cases. It was one that was important to blacks everywhere in the country.

Jewel LaFontant was the fourth generation of her family o attend Oberlin. Her great-grandmother, her grandfather, and her father were undergraduates there before her. A stop in the Underground Railway in the mid-nineteenth century, Oberlin College was one of the first colleges to admit students without regard to color. Women, too, were welcome here at an early date, for Oberlin was the first coeducational college in the United States.

After Oberlin, Mrs. LaFontant's grandfather, John Stradford, went on to the University of Indiana to study law and later settled in Tulsa, Oklahoma. In 1918, he was forced to leave the state. "There were ugly race riots and my grandfather was literally driven out of town," says Mrs. LaFontant. She offers it as an explanation for her ties to the Republican Party. "Friends have often asked me about my political affiliation," she says, "and I tell them that I inherited it." She notes that her father and grandfather, both of whom practiced law in Chicago, were very active in the Grand Old Party. "I've been in politics all my life," she says. She recalls that as early as age twelve, when her father ran for state representative, she was busy passing out petitions and literature. Over the years, she has often been asked about switching to the Democratic Party. "I've never considered it," she

says, "but even if I had, I certainly wouldn't have done i
in Chicago." She adds, with emphasis, "I'm just not a 'm
too' person."

Jewel LaFontant is close to the city of her birth and
graduate of its public schools—Willard Elementary and En
glewood High School. As a preteen, she competed in city
wide tournaments. In eighth grade, she placed second in
metropolitan tennis tournament that attracted dozens o
contestants. Always a good athlete, she remembers that fo
a time, she wanted to be a dancer. She also recalls that, dur
ing her elementary years, she performed acrobatics on stree
corners for money.

"I was the complete tomboy," she says, "and with good
reason." Disappointed in the very early marriage of a mucl
older brother, her father, Cornelius Stradford, treated Jewe
as a son. She recalls that he bought her suits—knickers and
jacket—which she wore to school during the elementary
grades. "I remember that once I had five of them," she says
"One was black, another brown . . . the others, navy, green
and gray. I don't think I owned a dress in those days." Sh
recalls that she did a lot of fighting and arguing and de
scribes herself as "Miss Tough." By high-school age, sh
had snapped out of this phase. At Englewood High Schoo
she played clarinet in the school band and earned severa
athletic letters.

Was her father responsible for her decision to study law
"I don't think so," she replies, "at least not directly." Sh
recalls that when she first told him of it, he took it rathe
lightly, to her surprise. Possibly it was because she was s
young. A friend of her years at Willard remembers tha
Jewel LaFontant talked about being a lawyer at the tim
they were in the fifth grade. Whatever their thoughts, th
family did not discourage her. Instead, they wisely contin

ied to instill confidence in the strong-willed young girl.
Remembering those early days, Jewel LaFontant says, "I
always felt I could do *anything*."

The childhood idea to study law stuck. Much later, she
reports, her father began to show great enthusiasm for it.
When it came time to make a decision about law school,"
she relates, "there were heated discussions." The burning
question was should she attend Columbia University Law
School in New York, her father's alma mater, or the University of Chicago. She decided on the latter, and Cornelius
Stradford accepted his daughter's choice in good grace. But
he was upset by her decision, upon graduation in 1946, to
marry her first husband, Chicago attorney, John Rogers, Jr.
For seven years, he did not speak to his daughter.

"My father was very strict," recalls Mrs. LaFontant. "During the years at home, I was not allowed to date. I was not
supposed to entertain callers until I was twenty-one years of
age." She remembers that she enjoyed the freedom of college life. At Oberlin, days were very busy. One of the first
women members of the Forensic Union, she took part in
these speaking events throughout her college days. For four
years, she was captain of the college volleyball team. "In
fact," she laughs, "I almost had a double major—political
science and physical education."

What does she recommend to young people today as a
pre-law major? She thinks that political science is fine, and
that economics is perhaps even better. She stresses the importance of learning social skills during school years. "It
doesn't matter how brilliant you are," she says, "if you can't
relate to people, they don't want you around."

Jewel LaFontant is, above all else, a realist. She candidly
admits that she has often been an "outsider." But she allows
herself no time for worry about it, and she has been phe-

nomenally successful at getting "on the inside." She makes i
sound simple. "I am a joiner," she confides, "and I mak
friends." She can talk matter-of-factly about the lunchtim
sit-ins that put a Chicago restaurant out of business. An
she can sit on boards with bankers called upon to financ
businesses. Jewel LaFontant says, "You can't accomplis
much on the outside." But she knows a lot about what ca
be done "on the inside."

"I have made many friends," she says, "through my wor
in professional, political, and civic organizations." She sus
pects that some of those ties were responsible for her ap
pointment, in 1955, to the position of Assistant U.S. Attorne
for the Northern District of Illinois. She was assigned to th
Civil Division of that office, where she handled many im
migration and deportation cases. She held this post until he
resignation in 1958.

She left the U.S. Attorney's office a few months prior t
the birth of John, her only child. But her resignation did no
signal a retirement from legal work. She simply moved bac
into private practice in a neighborhood on Chicago's Sout
Side in an office that she describes as "a lot more conv
niently located." She recalls that she was home for about
month at the time of John's birth and worked only part-tim
for a year or so. After that, she returned to the office an
was again in court on a regular basis.

Jewel LaFontant and her father had been reconciled i
the mid-1950s. Some years later, she and John Rogers, Jr
were divorced. In late 1961, Jewel married her second hus
band, attorney Ernest LaFontant. Together, they asked he
father to join them in a new law firm that was to becom
Stradford, LaFontant, Fisher & Malkin.

Cornelius Stradford practiced law in Chicago for mor

han forty years. He was one of the founders of the National
Bar Association, an organization in which Jewel served as
secretary for several years. The Stradford name was retained
by the firm long after Cornelius Stradford's death in 1963.

In addition to maintaining an active law practice with the
firm, Jewel LaFontant devoted hundreds of hours to work
in civic and professional organizations. She has had a fascinating and wide-ranging series of assignments and earned
an array of honors. She has served on countless bar association committees and is currently a member of the Board of
Editors of the *Journal* of the American Bar Association. A
member of the Economic Club of Chicago, she also serves
on the Board of WTTW (Chicago's public television station) and as a Director of the United Cerebral Palsy Association and a host of other philanthropic organizations. A
trustee of two colleges, she has received honorary degrees
from a half-dozen institutions of higher learning.

In June 1975, she was a Delegate to the International
Women's Year meetings in Mexico, and in October of that
year, she traveled to China as a guest of the People's Re-
public of China.

In the late 1960s, Jewel LaFontant began what was to be
a long and significant role in the corporate world. In 1969,
she was asked to serve on the Board of Directors of the
Jewel Tea Co. She recalls her mother's response. "Why
you?" asked the surprised Mrs. Stradford. "I didn't take
offense," says Mrs. LaFontant. "It was a natural question."
She recognizes that, as a woman and a black, she did not
fit the stereotype of the corporate director, particularly at
that time.

She no longer sits on the Jewel Tea Board, but in the
years following, she was asked to join the Boards of Direc-

tors of Transworld Airlines (TWA), the Bendix Corporation
Continental Bank, and Foote, Cone & Belding, the nation
ally renowned advertising firm.

Although questions like her mother's are less frequen
now, she admits that she is still asked "Why?" sometime:
She doesn't bridle, it is not her style. Attuned to people a
persons, Jewel LaFontant meets them unburdened by an
residue of resentment. Maturing in the liberal collegiat
community of Oberlin, Jewel LaFontant reflects anothe:
far gentler, era of racial integration.

That does not mean that she has not spoken out mo:
forcefully for equality. As a young practicing lawyer, sh
readily admits that discrimination cases occupied the lion
share of her time. As a student, she had proudly listened t
her father argue the important case in the U.S. Suprem
Court that was a forerunner of so many decisions in th
decades following. She has watched with satisfaction, to
the attainment of many of the goals her father and h
friends in the Congress of Racial Equality (CORE) fougl
for in decades past.

Does she think the fight to end racial and sex discrimina
tion is over? "By no means!" she says. But she thinks tha
blacks and women have reached a significant plateau. "W
have," she says, "won the right *to be there* . . . to sit i
key positions." But there is much more to be done, she say
once you are *in*. She makes a point not always acknowledge
"I am fully aware of the 'buddy system' and I know th
discrimination isn't limited to race and sex and that it ha
pens to other women and to men too, both black and white

Although Jewel LaFontant is tolerant and generous i
her appraisals of other human beings, she also emphasiz
the importance of being vigilant and alert to discriminato
acts. She cites an example from her days in the Solicito

ffice. One day, one of the secretaries in the office told her
hat the *men* in the office sometimes held meetings to which
Mrs. LaFontant was not invited. "It could have been a seri-
us matter," she says, "if you aren't there when decisions
re made, you get the worst of it." She went straightaway
o Robert Bork, then Solicitor General. She says that he
as shocked and that he dealt with her concern immedi-
tely. "After that," she laughs, "I was invited to so many
eetings that I sometimes wondered if I should have com-
ained."

That episode, triggered as it was by the tattling of a
yal secretary, reveals in yet another way the dimensions
f Jewel LaFontant's personality. She is genuinely admired
y other women. The women in her Chicago office who
anage her stenographic work and her complicated sched-
le are clearly devoted to her. Both feel that there are ad-
antages to having a woman for a boss. She has thoughtfully
ranged one secretary's hours so that she can leave at 3 P.M.
ch day to be at home when her young children return
om school.

In corporate boardrooms, she evokes the same warm re-
onse from many of the men who serve as fellow trustees.
metimes they sit together around the enormous file-laden
bles in New York or Chicago. On occasion, the meetings
e held in more exotic places. In May 1976, for example,
e meeting of the TWA Board was held on the island of
orfu.

Of course, the meetings themselves account for only a
action of Jewel LaFontant's work time on these corporate
ards. Prior to each meeting and throughout the month,
ick packages of materials arrive in her office. They con-
in reports, recommendations, and other documents needed
r decision making. All must be read before the meetings.

There is also committee work. The concerns of the audit an
consumer affairs committees on which she serves as a mem
ber of the TWA Board occupy many additional hours. Jewe
LaFontant estimates that she spends about two hundre
hours annually to meet her TWA Board responsibilitie
The work on each of the other boards consumes somewha
less time each year.

Does it bother her to work with all male, or largely ma
colleagues? "Not in the least," says Mrs. LaFontant, "afte
all, I have been doing it all of my life." She was graduate
from the University of Chicago in a class with only tw
other women. During most of the years of her practice, th
Chicago Bar has been a heavily male group as have bee
many of the civic organizations in which she has partic
pated over the years. In 1973, she received an award from
the Chicago YWCA as one of the city's six most outstandin
professional women. She might as easily have been hon
ored by the *male* arm of the "Y," for she served for yea
on the Board of the Maxwell Street YMCA.

Jewel LaFontant is at ease in the most imposing corporat
boardrooms of the country, and she is no less so in the inte
national arena. In 1972, she served as U.S. delegate to th
27th General Assembly of the United Nations. Her so
then thirteen, remembers best the small New York apar
ment. If John was impressed by the many celebrities he me
at the U.N., he doesn't recall. Of course, he was used
meeting well-known personalities because his mother kne
a great many of the prominent "movers" in Chicago lif
Former Governor of Illinois, Richard Ogilvie, is a friend a
is Reverend Jesse Jackson, Chicago's vocal black leade
whom she represented at one time. In 1972, Mrs. LaFontar
was elected Delegate to the Republican National Conver

ion, along with Ogilvie, U.S. Senator Charles Percy, and others. A *Chicago Tribune* photo taken at the Convention shows her seated next to insurance tycoon, W. Clement Stone.

Over the years of her growing professional commitments, Jewel LaFontant worked out a three-pronged solution to the problem of managing a household and caring for her young son. She says that neither of her husbands was especially eager to take on domestic chores. There was, however, a good bit of help from grandmother Stradford. There were paid helpers too, more as the family prospered. On many, many occasions, John was simply taken along to office or courtroom.

John remembers well the many hours he spent in the courtrooms of downtown Chicago. "I didn't mind going," he says, "because very often we went to a movie or had some other treat afterwards." Frequently, though, they had to wait a long time for his mother's case to be called. He remembers being very bored, and that it was sometimes hard to be quiet in court. During his younger years, he recalls, he and his mother played endless games of tic-tac-toe while waiting. When he was a bit older, he sometimes went out for candy or simply explored the building. He came to feel very much at home in Chicago's Daley Center, a vast building that confuses and awes many of the troubled hundreds who stand each day before the carefully banked elevators on their way to the courtrooms above.

With all that early exposure, is John interested in becoming a lawyer? He says "no." An economics major at an Ivy League school, John hopes to teach and to coach basketball at the college level. The potential is there. During his senior year of high school, he was named to the All-State team for

Class A schools in Illinois. He was also picked as a guard on the *Chicago Tribune* All-Area squad that year—one of fifty top players chosen from a highly competitive field.

Both parents have encouraged John in all his athletic ventures. When he was younger, John was sent to a camp in Wisconsin every summer where he excelled in a host of sports. As a teenager, John attended Dick Motta's basketball camp in Aurora, Illinois, for several summers. He credits much of his success in basketball to help he received at this unusual camp. Only six feet tall, John is short for basketball, but he has learned to hustle. His mother describes him as very competitive. She says he won't be satisfied to be "second-rate." That pleases her. John says that one of his problems, at first, was temper. With the help of Motta and his staff, he gradually learned not to get angry at referee calls that seemed unfair.

During the winters, John bowled in several leagues. He recalls that Mrs. Shelby, a housekeeper who was with the family for years, often chauffeured him to the bowling alleys and to other sports events. Both of his parents attended games as often as possible. "I was such a basketball booster at John's high school," says Jewel, "that even after he was graduated, the coach called and asked me to come to the games there." She adds that she also attended many of her stepson's games, especially during the period when her husband's two children by his former marriage lived with the LaFontants.

Jewel LaFontant confesses that her interest in John's welfare had everything to do with her life-style during the years in Washington, D.C. Spending week nights at her small apartment in the capital, she returned to Chicago most weekends. Her maternal role was also a factor in her decision to leave the Deputy Solicitor's job and return to private practice in the summer of 1975. "John's senior year was coming up," she recalls, "and friends told me it would be too bad to miss it . . . that once he was off to college, I would have lost my little boy."

Today, a modest, engaging young man, John credits his father with making sure he wasn't spoiled. "He set up very definite rules for me," says John. Mrs. LaFontant says that possibly she was a bit permissive—not because she was a working mother—but because her own father had been so strict. Since Mrs. LaFontant divorced John's father and remarried while John was quite young, his time with mother and father has always been divided. During most of the years, he lived with his mother and spent weekend time with his father, usually arriving on Saturday noon and going to school from there on Monday mornings. During the two years that Mrs. LaFontant was commuting from Washington, this pattern was often reversed so that she could be with him on weekends. Because she was able to work most evenings in the apartment in Washington, "homework" on weekends in Chicago was not heavy. When necessary, she used the law library at the University of Chicago Law School.

In 1974, Jesse Jackson publicly proposed that Jewel LaFontant run for mayor of Chicago. (She denies having had any interest in the post.) Some months later, she was among those spotlighted in a *Chicago Tribune* series on the most influential women in the city. The suggestion and the story are small details in the Jewel LaFontant saga, but they tell much about her stature and the esteem in which she is held by those who know, in the city where her now-international reputation was made. On seven different occasions, in seven different settings, Jewel LaFontant has stepped forward to receive tribute as *the* "Woman of the Year." The awards came from organizations with diverse goals. It is not surprising because Jewel LaFontant's admirers are a growing group, and one that cuts across all real or perceived lines of color or class.

SOIA MENTSCHIKOFF

Commercial Law Authority; Law School Dean; Professor

When the new University of Miami Law School building was being constructed, Dean Soia Mentschikoff was given a "hard hat." She claims that she spent no time on the scaffolds. If she did not scramble aboard the swaying platforms of the superstructure, it was the only thing she did not do to keep the giant project moving. On July 1, 1974, she became Dean. Eight months later, construction began; nine months hence, in December 1975, it was completed. It was a formidable feat—and a tribute to the talent of the new Dean as an expediter. Like construction projects the world over, the undertaking was threatened with delays. On more than one occasion, supplier's promises seemed to dissolve like Jell-O in the Florida sun. When such crises loomed, the Dean got on the telephone. Her success awed the contractors and amazed her staff. Says her admiring assistant, Mrs. Frances Shea, a veteran of twenty-five years of service in the

101

Miami Law School office, "She just knew how to get things done."

Longtime friends of the Dean were less surprised. Known among them for years as a persuader par excellence, the Dean's activities brought chuckles and comments that the only new feature was the site.

Most of them would recall that the Dean earned her professional reputation during the 1950s when she persuaded dozens of the nation's top lawyers to push for the adoption, in their respective states, of the new Uniform Commercial Code that she had helped to write. Eventually adopted by all states except Louisiana, the Code was a monumental revision and standardization of a hodge-podge of widely varying state laws that had snarled, and sometimes scuttled business transactions throughout the United States.

In charge of the huge Commercial Code project was Columbia University Law Professor Karl Llewellyn, whom Soia married in 1946. As Associate Chief Reporter, Soia was Llewellyn's chief assistant and a principal drafter of the Code. The sweeping project involved a host of individuals, of course. But following its completion in the late 1940s, Soia became the leading spokesperson for the newly crafted document. For some years, she was the number one salesman for the Code, covering a countrywide circuit. She met with both legal scholars and practicing lawyers to explain, and sometimes debate, the merits of the various new provisions. Some of the proposals represented departures from existing law. Most of the recommended changes were attempts to bring unity to the commercial laws of the various states. With the growing emphasis on national marketing and organization, the reforms were urgently needed by both the business community and the consumers of its products and services.

The Dean describes the period during which she was functioning as advocate for the Code as akin to the administrative process wherein rules are promulgated, comments received, and responses made. "Of course," she says, "the meetings and conferences were not formal hearings." After its adoption by the state of Pennsylvania in 1951, the Code was on its way to wide acceptance. However, almost immediately, committees were formed to work on refinements or modifications of the provisions. As a member of the permanent editorial board, Soia was active in this work for many years.

The work on the U.S. Commercial Code project took Soia Mentschikoff to all parts of the country. In the discussions and debates, her superior skills were placed in plain view of some of the nation's foremost lawyers and legal educators. It was not long before the praise of her legal talent became a chorus. Her reputation carried her, from 1947 to 1949, into the halls of Harvard where, as a Visiting Professor, she became the first female ever to teach in that venerable law school. In 1951, she and her husband, Karl Llewellyn, joined the law school faculty at the University of Chicago. She served as professor there until Miami beckoned in 1974.

The Chicago decades were busy ones. Until his death in 1962, Soia was a devoted wife, confidante, professional collaborator, and hostess for her husband Karl. Some years senior to Soia, who was his fourth wife, he came to Chicago with a long-established reputation as one of the nation's leading legal scholars. Soia calls Karl a genius. A gregarious man, he was also an inveterate host, long accustomed to entertaining both colleagues and students in his home on a regular basis.

In Chicago, Soia was called upon to keep intact both a

complicated household and a huge old home not far from
the campus. Soia's parents, who lived upstairs, moved to
Chicago with the Llewellyns. A few years later, Soia's
brother was divorced and moved to the West Coast, leaving
his two small daughters with their frail mother in rural North
Carolina. For some years, the girls spent summers with
Soia and Karl. In 1958, they moved to Chicago to live with
the Llewellyns and attend the Laboratory School at the
University of Chicago. Nieces Jeanne and Sandy Mentschikoff were then aged nine and ten.

Through it all, during the 1950s and 1960s, Soia was forg-
ing her career. She was teaching commercial law, procedure, and other courses at the University of Chicago Law
School. She also worked on the Code revisions and supervised an ambitious Commercial Arbitration project. She
wrote a casebook on commercial law, co-authored a book
on international law, and published numerous other materials.

Incredibly, the list of her other contributions to the profession made during this time is also long. She was a Com-
missioner (representing Illinois) on Uniform State Laws
and a member of the American Law Institute. She served as a
director of the National Legal Aid and Defender organization and council member of the National Endowment for
the Humanities as well as a member of the Commission on
the Rights, Liberties and Responsibilities of American In-
dians. She was a council member of the Society of International Law and a consultant to the Agency for International
Development (AID). Over the years, she was a member of
bar association committees beyond count at local, state, national, and international levels.

Soia Mentschikoff's legal career is impressive by any
standard and it was, it appears, a career that was long in the

planning. The Dean says that she became interested in studying law when she was about ten years old. She recalls that she found evidence of this once when she discovered some old papers on which she and a friend had, years earlier, written their career choices. She believes that her decision may have been influenced by the news stories of Clarence Darrow's role in the Scopes trial, which took place about this time. The Dean was born in 1915, in Moscow, because business had taken her American parents to that city. However, they returned to New York when Soia was three years old, and she was educated in the public schools of New York City.

At Hunter College, Soia developed speaking skills by taking an active role in campus politics, and she honed her writing ability by doing columns for the college newspaper. Today, as the Dean of a leading United States law school, she is often asked what she recommends to students as a pre-law major. She doesn't tout any particular course of study. She favors courses in which students learn to make an orderly presentation of ideas. She suggests that students take a variety of courses that require different kinds of writing. She believes that journalism courses can be very useful. She stresses that, "Any student planning to go to law school should enroll in courses in which lengthy papers are required." Classes in speech and debate, the Dean points out, can also help students learn to organize ideas and present them.

Soia Mentschikoff was captain of the Hunter College basketball squad. Over the years, she has had enthusiasm at times for golf, bicycling, and various other athletic activities. A tall woman and sturdily built, she often talks of dieting and occasionally does. For many years, her favorite pastime has been walking. It is fine exercise, she says, but more than that, the walks are a prime time for meditation and renewal. A magnetic personality, the Dean enjoys people, but she also cherishes the solitary hours that the long walks provide. Asked the chief challenge of her job as Dean, she chuckles and says, "Finding enough time to get to the beach."

She received her undergraduate degree from Hunter College at age nineteen, finding enough time apart from activities to compile an academic record that brought a fellowship and admission to the Law School of Columbia University.

Although Soia's parents were neutral about this new venture, she began law school with great enthusiasm and the resolution—not always kept—to attend classes regularly. As a Columbia law student, she also began to attend the weekly "at homes" for students that were hosted by Professor Llewellyn. During her second year of law school, she secured a paying job as Llewellyn's assistant, helping him with assorted scholarly chores. Sometime during her third year in law school, Llewellyn urged her to begin looking into possible jobs she might obtain upon graduation. Soia says that she was not, at that time, particularly worried about whether she would have difficulty in finding a position.

Her cool self-confidence in approaching the employment scene is confirmed by the audacity of her first act. Interested in litigation work, Soia contacted John W. Davis, a leading New York attorney and former Democratic presidential candidate. As one of the nation's foremost lawyers, Davis argued more than a hundred cases before the U.S. Supreme Court. During the forty-five-minute interview, Davis was cordial but he told her that, with one exception, women had not impressed him as litigators. He did, however, make arrangements for her to talk at a later date with another member of the firm. Incorrectly assuming that this individual was in a department of the firm in which she had no interest, she canceled the appointment and moved her job hunt to other terrain. (Sometime later, she found out that her guess had been wrong—the man headed the litigation staff—but by this time she had landed another job.)

Her next step in pursuing employment was equally bold, and it reveals much about her style. Following the Davis interview, she returned to the administration offices at the Columbia Law School. There she confronted Assistant Dean Gifford, then in charge of placement, with a request for letters of introduction to some fifty New York firms. She shrugs off questions about his ready compliance with her request. She notes that she was in the top ten percent of the class. "Besides," she says, "except for the addresses, they were form letters."

As it happened, forty-six of the letters were unnecessary. Soia had taken some course work in labor law, then a relatively new field, and she decided to pursue this special area of the law. She recalls that at one of the first firms she contacted relative to labor law work, she was told that they "did not hire women." Nonetheless, she says, the interview was helpful because the interviewer referred her to a smaller firm—Scandrett, Tuttle & Chalaire—where she got a job immediately. After a few years with this firm, she had a brief stint as general counsel to one of the companies the firm represented. In 1941, she joined the Wall Street firm later known as Spence, Hotchkiss, Parker & Duryee, where she was made a partner in 1944. During most of these years, she was also functioning as an assistant or associated reporter for a major law reform project. The first, the Uniform Revised Sales Act occupied her time from 1942 to 1944.

The Uniform Commercial Code work, which went on in one form or another for so many years, began in 1944.

Soia Mentschikoff was, at one time, sympathetic to a push to disband separate professional organizations for women but she has not played a visible role in the women's rights movement. She readily acknowledges that, for years, women were not warmly welcomed by the hiring partners of many law firms. She recognizes that sex discrimination in the employment of lawyers did, and does, exist. Asked if she ever experienced it, she replies, "Yes, but I've not been personally affected by it. . . ."

For the most part, Soia Mentschikoff as an individual appears to have dealt with the sex discrimination issue by attempting to ignore it. She believes that sometimes individuals may, by their own attitudes, generate problems for themselves. Stressing the vital role played by one's self image, she tells female law graduates that the appropriate thought pattern is: "I am a lawyer," not "I am a woman lawyer." She feels that whenever a female thinks of herself or is viewed by others, as a *woman* lawyer, one dimension has been taken from that person's professional status. "It is demeaning," she says.

In more ways than this, she strongly urges young people not to live up to "someone else's expectations." "Don't let people label you," she admonishes, "don't let them put a box around you." In recent years, she has become concerned about another trap. Increasingly, in her speeches, she devotes time to cautioning young people not to put a box around *themselves* either. She looks skeptically upon the popular game of seeking to "find oneself." Instead, she says, "People should remember that they are multidimensional. Each of you," she tells individual students, "is a lot of different people."

Soia Mentschikoff is a woman with a deep devotion to her church (Russian Orthodox) and to her family. She acknowledges that women often have hard choices to make. To the women who wish to combine careers and the rearing of children, she stresses the important role played by supportive spouses. Does she advise these women to look for such husbands? "No," she says, "I tell them to marry whomever they wish, but to recognize that there will be problems if the husband has more traditional expectations concerning their wifely role."

In discussing the pros and cons of a woman's dropping out for a time to meet family obligations, the Dean hedges. She feels that once legal competence or expertise has been established, it is feasible for women to make arrangements for more flexible hours that will enable them to spend more time at home. If a woman already has heavy family obligations at the time of graduation from law school and is unable to make a substantial initial time commitment to work outside the home, she says, then entry into the professional world may have to be delayed.

During the time that her nieces were living with her, Soia did a great deal of her work at home. Friends of those Chicago years recall that books and papers were stacked everywhere in the house. "The dining room table was usually completely covered. We would have to clear it off to make room to eat," says Jean Allard, a former student who visited often in the Llewellyn home.

Mrs. Allard, who is now a prominent Chicago attorney, later became general counsel to the Maremont corporation and a Vice President of the University of Chicago. Jean Allard cherishes the professional guidance Soia gave her. "She taught me everything about being an effective lawyer," says Mrs. Allard. She pays tribute to Soia's instinctive ability to identify the underlying problem in any given set of facts She says that Soia has a "strong sense of transactionalism" and an insight that makes her highly creative in working out superior solutions to legal problems. She notes too Soia's emphasis on the practical.

Jean Allard was the only female in the second-year law class when the Llewellyns came to Chicago in 1951. She recalls that she first met Soia in the law school restroom when the Llewellyns were visiting the campus the previous spring. Despite an impertinent greeting from the brash young student, they quickly became friends. Mrs. Allard recalls that for many years, there were few women at the law school and Soia always took a special interest in each of them. She also spoke, at times, to the wives of male students explaining to them the demands their husbands faced in the legal world.

Continuing the practice begun at Columbia, students were regularly welcomed at the Llewellyns' home. From fifteen to twenty-five students from Soia and Karl's classes were invited for cider and donuts and good conversation each Sunday night. Mrs. Allard was one of the scores of students befriended by the Llewellyns. Many were fiercely devoted to them, and they often helped with household chores. Mrs Allard recalls that, on one occasion, she agreed to feed the cat while the Llewellyns were in Cleveland for a week. Unfortunately, they forgot to leave a key. "I was seven months pregnant at the time," she says, "but I crawled through the window twice a day the entire time to feed the cat." Students were also, on occasion, drafted to care for "Happy," the small white poodle that was a birthday gift to niece Sandy and a family pet for many years.

Following her graduation from law school, Jean Allard shared an office at the University of Chicago Law School with Soia for five years. Among her tasks was assisting with the ambitious Commercial Arbitration project, which Soia had stocked with scholars from across the country. Work on this project took the Llewellyns one summer to New Mexico for special work with the Zia Indian tribe near Albuquerque. Niece Sandy Mentschikoff went along. In the summers following, both of the nieces spent a great deal of time with the Llewellyns in Chicago. After their move to Chicago in 1958, the girls visited in North Carolina in the summers.

Over the years of their growing up, Soia voluntarily undertook greater and greater responsibility for the care and education of her nieces. However, the girls called Soia and Karl by their given names, and the Llewellyns did not, at any point, assume parental roles. Jeanne recalls that her aunt was always concerned, but was not overly strict with the girls. Although their grades at school were very uneven, she doesn't remember any strong measures taken to bring improvement, except that television viewing was restricted to an hour a day on weekdays, and two hours a day on weekends. Sandy, who majored in political science at Lake Forest College, is now married to an economics professor and is the mother of a small son. Jeanne attended the University of New Mexico. A social worker for some years, Jeanne is now a student in the Chicago Kent College of Law. Jeanne says that Soia was very pleased with her decision to study law, but she did not push either of the girls toward a legal career.

During the years when the girls were living with the Llewellyns, grandmother Mentschikoff (called "mama-toy" by everyone) lived upstairs. She was available for baby-sitting, and the families dined together often. At least once a week, the girls went upstairs to eat dinner with their grandparents. Jeanne also recalls that during one period when Karl and Soia were very busy, they dropped the girls off each Saturday to spend long hours at Chicago's giant Museum of Science and Industry near the campus.

Karl welcomed the girls, and they took care not to disturb him when he was working at home. They remember him as a temperamental man and very devoted to Soia. On days when Soia slept in, Karl would bring her coffee and fix breakfast. (In later years, Soia began to rise very early in the morning, but she still maintains that she is basically a "night person.")

It was Edward Levi, later President of the University of Chicago and still later U.S. Attorney General, who brought the Llewellyns to Chicago. When he assumed the deanship of the University of Chicago Law School in 1950, he asked the faculty to name the individual they would most want to join the law school staff. The answer: "Karl Llewellyn." Mr. Levi recalls that when he began making inquiries about Llewellyn, he was greatly impressed by the number of laudatory remarks everyone made about Llewellyn's wife, Soia. He decided to make a place for her as well. He feels that in the beginning, Soia may have had some reservations about coming to Chicago. He is clearly pleased with his role in luring her to the Windy City, where she had so many happy and fruitful years.

Ed Levi and other friends and colleagues of their Chicago years recall that Karl never stopped singing Soia's praises. Kate Levi recalls that Karl told her, before she met Soia, that his wife could "do anything." The Levis soon joined Soia's coterie of admirers. "Soia has an extraordinary combination of abilities," says Ed Levi. "I've always told her . . . 'you are unfair to men because you have all they have, and so much more.'" His decision to offer her the position was nonetheless, a courageous one because at that time there were less than half a dozen women in the entire country who had teaching professorships in the law schools.

For many years, the Levis lived less than a block away from the Llewellyns. They visited often in each other's homes. Kate Levi recalls Soia's telephone call on that terrible night in 1962 when Karl died so unexpectedly. In fact, the Llewellyns had been invited to dinner at the Levis that very evening and Karl, feeling indisposed, had gone home earlier than Soia. All of the Llewellyn's friends of those days recall the deep and prolonged grief Soia experienced. For some time, they feared for her health.

The marriage had been a truly remarkable one, a union that brought happiness at the deepest level. Karl, a scholar with an unbelievably broad background, was Soia's mentor in the professional world in the early days. Beyond that, Karl's devotion seems to have provided a kind of vital ballast for Soia. She has said, on occasion, that if all is well in one's personal life, there is no end to what he or she can accomplish professionally.

Perhaps one of the key elements in the success of Soia and Karl's relationship was their sensitivity. According to Jeanne, they were always careful about treading into areas that might be especially hurtful to the other. They took care to spare the girls' feelings too. Jeanne recalls that, as teenagers, she and Sandy were often careless about keeping the house in order when the Llewellyns were away. Years later, she learned that the travelers always took pains not to surprise the girls on their return. Whenever possible they would call ahead before departing so the girls could put things back together. If they failed to reach them from the point of departure, they deliberately dallied at the airport in Chicago.

On the other hand, Soia's concern for the girls also led her, at times, to reach into their lives in traditional motherly ways. When Sandy was married, Soia supplied much of the furniture for the young couple's apartment, along with generous bits of advice about where it should be placed in each room. Soia was there too when Sandy's baby was born. Describing the event to friends, she respectfully recited some of the old superstitions regarding childbirth. It was not the first time they had heard her speak in this vein. Though it seems in stark contrast to a mind so steeped in reason, the mystical is a part of Soia Mentschikoff too.

The Dean is not effusive, nor a gladhander. Her speeches, which she never writes out in full, tend to be a bit rambling. The details of her appearance—her hair, makeup, and dress —don't rate a high priority in her life. She is quiet of voice, yet others draw near. A skillful politician, she has a strong, intuitive wisdom that guides all of her contacts with people. In one-to-one encounters, she captivates; in small groups she rapidly builds rapport. Always, she exhibits a sense of being "in control." "At parties," says Jean Allard, "the men flock to her side."

In 1973, the largely male membership of the prestigious Association of American Law Schools (AALS) named her president-elect of that organization. In 1974, she became president. The AALS is the "voice" and unifying organ for more than one hundred and fifty law schools. With law school enrollments during her tenure burgeoning to well over one hundred thousand students, the legal establishment was called upon to meet a host of new challenges.

Asked to name the most significant achievement during her term of office, she cites the initiation of separate annual meetings—one for recruitment of teaching staff and one for scholarly presentations. She notes that the recruiting, which intensified over those years of vast growth, began to intrude upon the educational functions of the annual gathering. The move to hold two meetings was a simple, sensible solution.

More recently, Soia Mentschikoff's practical bent has been a boon to all those involved in learning, or teaching, or planning, or finance, at the University of Miami Law School. In her personal life something of a procrastinator, the Dean keeps things moving as an administrator. Blessed with some quantum of impatience, some intolerance for the shoddy and the incomplete, she is action-oriented. And when she acts, she gets results. She knows whom to call; persuading them to act is perhaps her finest talent. Strangers bend to her pleas; so do friends. Nor does she hesitate to reach out to her vast array of friends, former students, and professional acquaintances to ask for help when it is needed.

Just now, she is occupied in building a great law school. Construction was a part of the task. But there are many other components of the premier institution she expects to establish in Miami. Soia is immersed in an all-out effort, one that requires a heavy commitment on the part of the Dean and a great many of the other individuals who will eventually make it go.

Soia Mentschikoff's energies are considerable. She used to keep late hours, toiling far into the night to complete pressing projects. Now, she is most often up each day at dawn or before. She uses these quiet hours for study at home each morning before she leaves for the office.

A large chunk of the Dean's weekly work time of sixty hours or more is devoted to planning or implementing particular programs at the law school. The Law and Economics Institute was opened in 1974. Also associated with the law school now is the Center for Interdisciplinary Studies, a vehicle for exploring the impact of law on human behavior.

Three times each week, the Dean heads for a large class-room where she guides freshman law students through a course titled, "Elements of Law." A survey course, it does not require extensive preparation. Much of her day—fifty percent, by her own estimate—is spent in meetings of one kind or another.

Soia Mentschikoff began coming to Miami in the late 1960s. She served as a Visiting Professor at the Law School for some years immediately prior to assuming the deanship. Soia Mentschikoff has had time to think, during all the years of long walks along the Florida beaches, about what Miami's new "Tower of Excellence" could be. Now that the mortar is dry and program plans are on the Dean's agenda for action, many of her friends would say that her goals are as good as made.

Although Soia is a brilliant legal theoretician, the practical is never far from her fingertips. She is famed for her skill in assessing the realities of a business transaction. She is equally shrewd in judging the human dimension. She says that when she finishes "deaning," she is going to write a volume on the elements of decision making. It's a book to look forward to.

BETTY SOUTHARD MURPHY

Labor Lawyer; Press Counsel; Chairman,
National Labor Relations Board

The voice disarms the visitor. Not theatrical, not booming, Betty Murphy's voice is low and exceedingly pleasant. "Let's sit here," she motions. She steers the visitor to a corner table, away from the huge desk that dominates the office she has occupied since February 1975, when she took over as Chairman of the National Labor Relations Board (NLRB). Assuming command of an agency charged with administering the most crucial federal labor laws and chairmanship of the five-member Board commissioned to wrestle with the thorniest cases, Betty Murphy became, in effect, the number one "keeper of the peace" on the labor relations front in the United States—and the first woman to sit in this hot seat.

A diverse group had gathered to watch Mrs. Murphy sworn in by President Ford on that wintry day. There were attorneys from the Washington law firms with which she was associated for fourteen years, and colleagues from her stint at the NLRB in the late 1950s, as well as fellow workers from

117

her preceding post as chief of the all-powerful Wage and Hour Division of the U.S. Department of Labor. Also present were her children, Ann and Cornelius, Jr. (then seven and six), her husband, Dr. Cornelius Murphy, and Estavia Rodriguez, friend and longtime housekeeper to the Murphys.

In discussing her good fortune in managing career and family, Betty Murphy has generous words for both Estavia and Dr. Murphy. Not present at the swearing-in was another person whom she credits with playing a major role in her success, her late mother, Thelma Casto Southard. Widowed when Betty was four years old, Mrs. Southard reared three small children, Betty and two brothers. Her genius, according to Mrs. Murphy, was that she managed not simply to feed and clothe them, but to instill in them a remarkable faith in themselves.

"My mother's unceasing refrain was that we could do anything if we had *confidence*," Betty Murphy says. "And she always told us that we were 'very special.'" Betty's brother Samuel, now a busy pediatrician in Atlantic City, New Jersey, laughs about it. He says, "By the time we found out that we weren't so special, we were successful." Mrs. Murphy laughs too, but her tone is earnest when she talks about her mother's influence.

Betty Murphy's great-grandfather, Samuel Southard, had been a U.S. Senator. The family was respected, but not wealthy. "Our monetary resources were quite limited," she says, "but mother encouraged us in countless ways." Mrs. Murphy recalls that when she was in seventh grade she had an assignment to write about her vocation goals, and she picked law. Her mother's input was to urge Betty to interview several local lawyers. Did these chats with members of the Bar inspire her to pursue the law? "Hardly," she smiles,

"One woman lawyer said to me, 'You'll just end up as a secretary, so you might as well go to business school.' "

The summer when Betty was fourteen, she saw in the help-wanted columns an ad for a job as a reporter on the local newspaper. She was eager to apply. "Instead of telling me that I was too young and inexperienced," she says, "Mother was very enthusiastic. She helped me to get dressed and primed to go and see the editor."

"Of course," she says, "I didn't get the job . . . but the editor was very respectful. He asked if I planned to return to school in the fall. When I said 'yes,' he said the reporting job might not work out." But her bold request did lead to the opportunity to sell classified advertising for the newspaper, a job that she worked at, on and off, during all of her high school years. The pay was good—at one point she recalls making as much as eighty dollars a week.

The money Betty earned was very welcome in the Southard household. But she counts the work experience and the boost to her growing self-confidence as much more valuable. She identifies self-confidence as the single most important ingredient in whatever success she has been able to achieve. She confesses to making a major effort to nurture this confidence in her own children. There is some evidence that she is succeeding. Recently, nine-year-old Ann announced that she probably would go to graduate school at Harvard.

Mrs. Murphy's serious interest in law came later, after some years abroad, study at the Sorbonne, and the pursuit of a variety of jobs, many unrelated to the undergraduate degree in Oriental Studies that she received from the Ohio State University in 1952.

When she returned to the United States in 1955, after a three-year work-study sojourn to Europe and Asia, she

headed for Washington, D.C. After a dogged effort, sh
finally landed a job with United Press International (UPI
in that city. It was at the UPI office that she heard a rumo
that the assignment of covering the U.S. Supreme Cour
might be opening up. She decided to take some courses a
the Law School of American University. "I thought," sh
confesses, "that this would give me an edge when the tim
came for the UPI Vice President to fill this spot."

It didn't work out that way. Instead, she became en
chanted with the law. "The day came when I had to choose
Would I be a reporter with a legal background? Or a lawye
with a newspaper background?" She chose the latter and sh
says that she has not had a remnant of regret about the de
cision. Once embarked on the legal path, did she ever view
the intervening years as wasted? "Never," she says, and ther
is no hesitation in her reply.

Gazing at her and listening to her decisive tone, the visi
tor's doubts vanish too. Mrs. Murphy is an attractive, per
suasive woman, solidly built and with clear features tha
match the crystal tones of her voice. She doesn't fuss ove
makeup, strands of her brown hair occasionally escape fron
their moorings, her dress is casual. But the resolution and th
sense of inner-direction are obvious. Even in a low-key con
versation, there is an orderly return to the main subject afte
each digression, showing a sharp mind.

Without comment or pause, she spells out for the visito
key names that come up in the conversation—a thoughtfu
by-product of her own newspaper days. She speaks of thos
days and says, without equivocation, "For the law, news
paper work is the best background. I learned to write quickl
and with precision." Early on, it appears, she was able t
write or dictate almost anything in final form. It is a rar
and valuable skill. "Occasionally," she says, "some mind

hanges may be made, but I don't go through several drafts,
r spend time rewriting."

She may ask staff members for background material, but
he writes her own speeches. Every year, there are many of
hem. She confesses that over the years, she has stood at the
odium for hundreds of hours just talking to young people.

Does she advise them to study law? Would she advise her
wn daughter to do so? "By all means," she says. She knows
he awesome statistics about the numbers of students en-
olled in law school today, but she thinks they will find jobs.
It may be that not all of them can go into private practice,"
he says, "but legal training will help them in many other
bs."

Would she advise those planning to go to law school to
ake the major she chose as an undergraduate? She laughs
nd explains that the "Oriental Studies" choice was random,
ut that her fascination with the Far East has persisted. She
as, for a time, a free-lance writer in the Orient. She has
cquired a collection of Buddhas that now numbers over a
undred. She glances at the large bronze Buddha that looks
npassively upon the comings and goings in her office. The
uddha rests on a shelf by a door that swings open and
ut unceasingly throughout the day, mocking the contem-
lative gaze. "No," she says thoughtfully, "I don't recom-
end a particular major for pre-law. The college years are
recious. I advise students to study whatever interests them."
he values her varied experiences. "I would do almost every-
ing I did all over again," she confesses.

What about the extracurricular activities in which she was
immersed during most of her student days? How impor-
nt are they in the scheme of preparation for law school?
etty Murphy was an active member of her sorority, Delta
elta Delta, as well as involved in a host of other activities,

in spite of having jobs that often cut sharply into her spare time. At Ohio State, where, even in the early 1950s the student body was over twenty thousand, she was one of the twenty coeds tapped for membership in Mortar Board, the national senior honorary that was, until recently, limited to women. The previous year she had been President of Chimes, the junior women's honorary. Membership in both groups was awarded for scholarship and significant service to the university community.

"I think activities are important," says Betty Murphy, "but I advise young people to concentrate on one organization to attain a role that will give them valuable leadership experience."

Does she encourage her children to join groups? "Not at their ages," she says. "We aren't much for the highly organized activities for very young children." The children who attend a private school, are sent off each morning to Estavia, long after Dr. and Mrs. Murphy have left the house for their respective jobs. Dr. Murphy, a radiologist at the Veterans Hospital, checks in very early and spends busy days with a never-ending stream of patients that require diagnostic screening. He says that he generally skips lunch and is home by about 4:30 P.M.

At the NLRB, Mrs. Murphy works incredibly long hours. As Chairman, she checks in at her office about 6:20 each morning and works until around 7 in the evening. Most often, she skips breakfast, though she may have coffee sometime later in the morning. Surprisingly, this self-assured superwoman doesn't like to drive. Although she keeps her driver's license up to date, she seldom is at the wheel. Nor does she use the limousine service that is available to her. Instead, she hitches a ride to work with Dr. Murphy in the mornings and rides home each evening with Ingrid Annibale, her secretary, who comes in around 9 A.M. each day.

Ingrid, who is also a working mother, has been Mrs. Murphy's secretary off and on for many years, and is a good friend as well. Their children, who are about the same ages, play together. This says much about Betty Murphy's relationship to her staff. Relaxed, sensitive, and highly respectful, she engenders in them a deep loyalty that is apparent even to the casual visitor. Tom Miller, NLRB Director of Communications, finds her especially appreciative. He is glad too for her newspaper background, which helps her to understand some of the limitations he operates under in getting agency news to the public.

Among those Betty Murphy lured to the NLRB is administrative assistant, Earl Proctor, an articulate black with a record of solid success in management in private industry. Proctor served as Executive Secretary to the Task Force appointed by Mrs. Murphy early in her administration. Stocked with representatives from both labor and management, the Task Force designed a plan that reduced the serious time lags in the handling of NLRB cases. Does Proctor mind that his "boss" is a woman? "Not at all," he says. He gives her top marks as an administrator and says her "human relations" skill is superb.

Does Betty Murphy herself feel that her sex has ever hampered her in advancing her career? "I do know that discrimination exists," she says, "but I have been *lucky*. I do not think it has ever touched me." On closer questioning, it becomes clear that her "luck" was accompanied, over the years, by considerable legwork and lots of sweat.

Betty Murphy's former law partner, Warren Woods, says that he discovered very quickly that Betty was a "real workhorse . . . a lawyer who worked rapidly, analytically, and well." It is clear that she is a person of considerable energy In addition to her demanding chores at the office and a home, she has served on countless bar association com mittees, and as trustee for several educational institutions.

Mrs. Murphy says that she does not remember worrying in law school about whether she would be able to get a job as a lawyer when she was graduated. Apparently, any energy that might have been consumed in worry was devoted in stead to tapping on legal doors all over Washington, D.C.

"I applied everywhere," she says, ticking off a list that in cluded law firms as well as most major government agencies She advises students today to do this—not to limit them selves—and with good reason. Her own efforts produced a unbelievable harvest—fourteen job offers. It was a phenome nal figure for the year 1958, especially since it included four offers from law firms that were not, in those days, quick t open arms to women law graduates.

Two offers especially attracted her, one from the NLR and one from the law firm of Roberts & McGinnis. She con sulted with the late William Roberts, senior partner, about her choice. He advised her to take the NLRB job. "You wi learn," he said, "how government works." Following his ad vice, she spent eighteen months at the NLRB and the joined the Roberts firm as an associate.

How does she now feel about that early stint in govern ment service? Did it bring the expected benefits? "It was wonderful experience," she says, "but I made one mistak I should have stayed longer. I recommend to young atto neys that they work at least three years in such positions." is a suggestion to be respected considering the level of train ing that Mrs. Murphy did get in the brief period when sl worked in the Appellate Court branch at NLRB, the ar sponsible for arguing cases in the U.S. Circuit Courts to obtain enforcement of NLRB decisions.

She recalls that her first argument was in a case before the U.S. Court of Appeals for the Seventh Circuit, sitting in Chicago. Was she nervous, that first time? "No," she says. "I had prepared the case from every possible angle and felt I knew my argument thoroughly. But I did have a problem— I got there and realized that I didn't know on which side of the courtroom I should sit." Laughing, she continues, "I relaxed when I saw opposing counsel arrive, thinking I would simply go to the table he didn't occupy. Unfortunately, we walked in together and he, being a gentleman, opened the gate and I had to precede him. Of course, I chose the wrong side and someone from the bench growled. But I won the case."

On another occasion, she recalls, she had to argue both sides of a case. Word reached the Court just minutes before Betty Murphy began her argument that opposing counsel was unable to proceed on account of an accident. When she finished, she was asked if she would be kind enough to present the opponent's position for the court. She recalls arguing vigorously and fully—"I knew the holes in my own case," she says—and then worrying, on the train going back to Washington, about the final result. Her supervisor was comforting, "Either way, you can't lose." The NLRB won.

For all of the valuable experience, Betty Murphy says that she felt ill-prepared and worked extremely hard in the early days at the Roberts firm. This probably accounts for what Woods describes as her "very high degree of client acceptance." This is a special tribute, he notes, because as a labor lawyer, she was working with some "macho" males in the packing industry. They were won over, Woods feels, by her skill and tenacity. He recalls that as a management represen-

tative during a particularly rough strike, her toughness stoo
her in good stead. For in those weeks, she was often in th
local court in connection with charges stemming from bruta
assaults or the hurling of ugly obscenities.

Woods notes too that Betty Murphy was, early on, activ
in litigation arising from the laws and regulations admini:
tered by the Equal Employment Opportunities Commissio
(EEOC). First involved at the appellate level in a cas
Woods had handled in a Louisiana district court, she went o
to represent a number of clients on related matters. As A
junct Professor of Law at the Washington College of La
of American University, she taught a course dealing with th
subject.

Do women lawyers have to work *harder?* "There is n
question about that," she replies firmly. "Women simpl
must do more to advance at a rate comparable to men." Do
she think this is less true now than formerly? Will it be tru
in the future? She isn't sure, but she feels that discriminatio
won't simply vanish. On the other hand, Betty Murph
thinks that there are almost unlimited opportunities fc
qualified women. She advises women, in the strongest term
to become "better prepared." She believes that the pressur
of the past decade have, in some instances, put women i
positions for which they weren't prepared. She views this :
counterproductive.

"I would never," she says, "hire a woman who was n
qualified for a position." But this is not a problem, she say
because there are plenty of qualified women around. (Bett
Murphy does not worry much about the details of sex libera
tion. She prefers to be called chairman, rather than "chai
person" or "chairwoman," for example.)

What about the fortunes of women in government? Sh
quotes Jayne Spain, retired Vice Chairman of the U.S. Civ

ervice Commission, who said, "Things happen when women
re in charge, when they head agencies." Clearly, things
id happen at the NLRB after Betty Southard Murphy
ook over. She downplays her role, but the facts are impres-
ive. For the first time in forty years, a woman (Helen
einer) was appointed NLRB General Council. And four
f the five Assistant Councils serving members of the Board
vere women.

The men who work with Mrs. Murphy at the NLRB are
oosters too, as are former colleagues at the law firms where
he labored so long. Her work in private practice was in-
redibly demanding, but it brought fascinating contacts too.
Vorking long hours and traveling constantly, she became a
artner in the Roberts firm in a few years. Not long after-
vards, this firm merged with another firm. The resulting
rganization was McGinnis, Wilson, Munson & Woods; now,
Vilson, Woods & Villalon.

During the years in private practice, Mrs. Murphy's time
vas about equally divided between labor law matters and
vork with the press. She often represented reporters in cases
n which they sought to protect their sources. For many
ears, the firm represented syndicated columnist Jack An-
erson.

Anderson's former top aide, Les Whitten, who is author
lso of the Washington-based novel, *Conflict of Interest*,
nd other books, has the highest regard for Betty Murphy's
gal abilities. He recalls the occasions when Mrs. Murphy
vas consulted about problems related to the column. "Her
dvice was always practical, always on target," he recalls.
In my twenty-five years as a reporter, I've never seen her
natch in a First Amendment case," he adds. Were there ever
ny problems about her being a woman? Whitten can't recall
ny. "Betty commands respect," he says. Praising her de-

meanor, he says, "Although she can be tough—unbendin
even—she retains her pleasant, businesslike air."

Whitten calls Betty Murphy an "able rescuer" and back
up the tag with accounts of the times she came to his aic
Once, he received a subpoena to produce some tapes mad
during an investigation of certain claims regarding John F
Kennedy's assassination. He recalls that one Sunday after
noon, a statement was being taken in the case. Mrs. Murph
held firm in defending his rights throughout the afternoo
and won the day when the opposing counsel was frustrate
into exploding, "To hell with the First Amendment."

On another occasion, Whitten was jailed by the F.B.
when he was apprehended on Washington's Rhode Islan
Avenue loading suspicious cartons into his car. The six car
tons contained land records and other documents missin
from the Bureau of Indian Affairs. Indian Leader Han
Adams, a friend of Whitten, was returning them, and Whi
ten was helping, with the prospect of an exclusive stor
Taken to the regional F.B.I. headquarters, Whitten asked t
make one phone call. The party he called was Betty Murph
and he praises her role in the matter. A tough reporte
Whitten confesses that he was "scared" during the five hou
before he was released that afternoon.

Whitten remembers too the contempt proceedings begu
by Judge John Sirica in 1973 when Anderson began pul
lishing in the column portions of the transcripts of gran
jury proceedings in the Watergate cases. Speaking of th
work done by the firm in connection with this episod
Whitten says flatly, "Betty helped to save the column." H
notes that with the limited staff Anderson had at that tim
they could not have continued the column if Anderson an
Whitten had languished in jail on contempt charges.

Whitten was there when Betty Murphy was sworn in by
Justice Brennan in July 1974 as Administrator of the Wage
and Hour Division, a subempire within the U.S. Department
of Labor that is responsible for enforcement of the Fair
Labor Standards Act, the Equal Pay Act, and more than sixty
other key federal statutes. After the ceremony, Whitten
chatted with an F.B.I. agent who had done background investigation on the new division chief. He recalls the agent
saying, "I've seldom investigated anyone I developed more
liking for."

The years in private practice, from 1960 to 1974, were
busy ones for Betty Murphy professionally. But if life at the
office was often hectic, life at home during this period was
seldom without excitement, and it was steadily growing more
complex.

In 1965, the well-traveled woman from East Orange, New
Jersey, married Dr. Cornelius Murphy. "Corny," as he is
called by virtually everyone, is eight years her senior and
full of Yankee wisdom, gained as a hard-working youth in a
large New Hampshire family. Over the years, Dr. Murphy
has met a demanding work schedule and still managed to
step in whenever help was required at home. "My husband
believes," says Betty, "that if a man is secure in his mascu-
nity, there is nothing he can't do around the house." She
counts his attitude a key factor in her successful balance of
career and family. "I always tell women who are planning
to do this," she says, "to be sure to marry a cooperative
husband."

Betty Murphy, the career woman, won't even admit to
having any "impossible days," because she says that their
flexible arrangements at home have worked so well. "We've
never had lists of duties, or anything like that. The work

that needs doing is done by whoever is available. If I wal
past a wastebasket that needs emptying, I empty it; my hu
band does the same."

In their first year as parents, when Ann was a baby an
before there was a live-in housekeeper, schedules wei
shifted from time to time. If the day worker didn't come i
either Betty or Corny stayed home, whichever one coul
least afford to be away went to work. Dr. Murphy recalls i
least one day when he went to work very early and cam
home so that Betty could get down to her office in the afte
noon of the same day. Dr. Murphy confesses that today I
would adjust his schedule "if Betty's commitments r
quired it."

Other factors also figure in the success of Betty Murphy
career-family combination. "By the time Ann was born," sl
says, "I was a partner and could adjust my hours at the offic
to some extent." Incredibly, she recalls that she was abl
with just one extra bottle each day, to nurse both babies unt
they were three months old. "In those days," she says, "
went in a bit later and generally came home at four in th
afternoon."

How much time did she take off from work when tl
babies were born? "I was in the hospital eight days whe
Ann arrived, in part because I had never held a baby o
changed a diaper before, and I was getting a cram course i
motherhood from the nurses." Did the new role interfei
with professional life? It appears that there was scarcely
missed beat. Work from the office was brought in durin
both hospital stays. On one occasion, Ingrid came so th
Betty could dictate a brief that had to be filed.

When the babies came home, Dr. Murphy's medical trai
ing and his experiences in a large family were invaluable. I
addition to these talents, Dr. Murphy has long been in charg

of the household marketing and is an accomplished cook. When the Murphy's entertain—which is often—he prepares gourmet specialties for the crowd. When the children have birthday parties, he may take responsibility for the cake, while Betty decorates and emcees the games.

Nowadays, Estavia prepares the evening meal. "Before the children were in school," says Betty, "she was very busy with them. The cooking was done by one of us—again, not by set plan, but according to who was free."

What about the feeding or attention that young children sometimes need during the night? It appears that Ann was a model child, sleeping soundly at a few months of age. But Cornelius, Jr., who is called Neil, was a different kind of infant. His father recalls that he was well over a year old before he developed reasonable sleeping habits. "We got lots of advice," Dr. Murphy recalls. "Betty's brother, the pediatrician, said, 'Let him cry!' . . . an edict easy to pronounce one hundred and fifty miles away, harder to live with." He continues. "Someone else suggested that solid food would help. We mixed it to the consistency of concrete, but it worked no magic." Like so many frustrated parents, Dr. Murphy utters the refrain, "If Neil had been the first, there would have been no others." Both children do well in school, but Neil remains the more boisterous and aggressive.

"Weekends," says Mrs. Murphy, "are reserved for the children. They take turns in selecting the restaurant we'll visit for our Saturday lunch." Neil generally chooses "Roy Rogers" hamburgers, while Ann often opts for Chinese food. When the latter is served, both mother and daughter eat it with chopsticks.

Sundays, and every other Saturday, are days-off for Estavia. If there are no houseguests, Dr. Murphy might fix breakfast for the children, letting Betty catch up a bit on rest after her arduous seventy-hour week. Nowadays, Es tavia sometimes gets up at night on the rare occasions whe the children need attention. Devoted to the Murphys, sh tries to help them conserve their energies.

Betty Murphy readily agrees that good housekeepers ar a treasure, and as hard to find. In choosing such a person, sh says flatly that the number one priority is that they be "ex cellent with children." The house comes second. She ha never made use of day-care facilities. The Murphy childre have been brought to the office on only one occasion that sh can recall.

There would be little to interest Ann and Neil at Mr: Murphy's office. It is likely too that even with their youthfu vigor, they would run out of steam trying to keep pace wit their energetic mother as she moves through a fully schec uled thirteen-hour day. She says, too, that she takes home full briefcase most evenings, and about five hours of catch-u reading somehow gets done on weekends. Travel for Mr: Murphy is less frequent now, but one or two trips a mont are often on the agenda. "I did so much of it for so man years," she says, "it is a pleasure to be able to spend mor time at home now."

Although travel time may be reduced, Betty Murphy hardly closeted in her office or in the boardroom at th NLRB. To do the best job for the agency, she finds it nece: sary to attend many conferences and meetings at othe government offices and on Capitol Hill. In her office, mee ings are often on the agenda too. Believing that they ofte waste time, Mrs. Murphy makes an effort to hold them to minimum. "Sometimes, if I'm rushed and a group comes i I just stand and remain standing. If they can't sit down, find that they leave more quickly," she says. This gambit i however, only a partial solution to the problem of cuttin

lown time spent conferring. Each day about forty or fifty
persons try to reach the chairman via telephone.

As Chairman, Mrs. Murphy spent about eight hours a
day on administration of the agency and about five hours
 day on the cases she handled as a working member of
the five-person Board. Cases come to the NLRB under
the terms of the National Labor Relations Act. Most fall into
ne of two categories—complaints about unfair labor prac-
ices that affect individuals, and decisions related to employee elections and the circumstances under which a union
ecomes bargaining agent. Twice a week—in sessions that
ast from 9:30 A.M. to noon—the Board meets to consider
ases. However, only the knottiest problems, about five per-
ent of all cases, reach the Board for review of decisions
nade by hearing officers or administrative law judges. The
ast majority of the cases are handled in the regional offices.

The docket of cases filed with NLRB—about 55,000 in
977—has increased 50 percent in the past decade. The time
lapsed in handling them has also been an increasing prob-
m. One of Betty Murphy's early priorities as NLRB chair-
nan was to try to reduce the time required to dispose of
ases filed with the NLRB. At the time she took office, the
verage time for the full process was over a year. Her goal
vas to reduce the time to six months. To meet the goal, she
ppointed the Task Force and the implementation of their
ecommendations resulted in a promising start. In her first
ear as chairman, productivity increased dramatically.

Betty Southard Murphy is in a unique position to meet her
esponsibilities at the NLRB in an evenhanded manner be-
ause she has had experience in representing both labor and
nanagement. Traditionally, labor lawyers tend to work for
ither labor *or* management. Even Board positions at the
NLRB are so divided—with two pro-labor seats and two pro-

management seats. As the chairman of the five-membe
Board, Betty Murphy drew praise from both sides dur
ing her tenure. It is a tribute to both her personal and he
professional skills.

ELISABETH OWENS

Professor of Law, Harvard University;
Director of Research, International Tax Program

I've always had a low tolerance for being discontented,"
says Betty Owens. The comment is perhaps a key to the pattern of her career—a steep upward spiral that has taken her
from journeyman economist for the United States government to a full professorship as Henry Shattuck Professor of
Law on the Harvard Law School faculty.

For Betty Owens, "discontent" has brought a lifetime sequence of exciting assignments. In 1940, she was graduated
summa cum laude from Smith College. Within the decade
following, she pursued graduate studies at the University of
Chicago, performed groundbreaking labors in helping to organize the Office of Price Stabilization (predecessor agency
to the OPA), and held a host of other challenging positions
in wartime Washington, D.C., that led her, in 1948, to the
doors of the Yale Law School.

Her record in the decade after her 1951 graduation from
Yale Law School is equally impressive. It included a four-

year stint with a respected Boston law firm and the begin
nings of her spectacular work in the field of internationa
law.

Working under Director Stanley Surrey, the renowned
tax authority, in the early days of the Harvard-based In
ternational Tax Program (ITP), and later with the pres
ent ITP Director, Harvard Professor Oliver Oldman, Bett
Owens performed with distinction a series of successivel
more exacting roles. She edited and wrote scores of material
published by the United Nations-affiliated ITP, and helped
with the training of students and tax officials attracted to the
program from nations around the world. In 1964, she wa
appointed Director of Research for ITP and a Lecturer in the
Harvard Law School. By 1967, when Professor Oldman too
a sabbatical leave for a semester, Betty Owens was able to
"run the show" at ITP.

In 1972, Betty Owens became the first woman to be ap
pointed full professor on the Harvard Law School faculty
It is a highly prestigious and coveted post. But it was, in a
way, a surprising tribute for a woman who had, early on
decided she "did not want to teach." By the time she wa
named professor, of course, Betty Owens had been a lecture
on the Harvard Law School staff for several years, and she
was a recognized authority on international tax law. She wa
well known for a number of major contributions to the field
most notably for a 1961 book entitled *The Foreign Ta*
Credit. A six-hundred-page volume outlining a host of com
plex laws, it has been described by some tax specialists a
the best single book written about tax law in the past thirty
years.

Chatting with the scholarly Professor Owens in her book
filled office at Harvard, the visitor stares in disbelief when
she says that as a high schooler at the Girls Latin School i

Boston she was not particularly interested in her studies. Ironically, her memories of high school center instead on her roles on two of the school's athletic teams—basketball (she played forward) and field hockey. She also recalls that she thought that one of the best things about the Latin School was the 2 P.M. dismissal time. On spring afternoons, she hurried over to nearby Fenway Park to watch the Boston Red Sox baseball games. In the fall, she attended all of the football games at Boston's Wentworth Institute, where her brother was on the team.

When pressed, she admits that she must have been a "pretty good student" in spite of her attitude. A premier public school, Girls Latin drew the best students from elementary schools throughout Boston. Another indication that Betty Owens' student days were not spent entirely on the playing fields is that her graduation from Girls Latin brought a scholarship and admission to Smith College, a highly competitive institution.

At Smith, Betty Owens played soccer and water polo and pursued, with more enthusiasm, her studies in economics and her literary interests. She recalls that she was especially pleased when she won a literary prize there because such awards were seldom given to students who were not English majors. At Smith, she recalls, she also helped to found a literary-political magazine. In those late depression years, she teamed up with a group of politically-oriented students who were eager to launch a new publication. "They were interesting people," she says. "I didn't share their zeal for politics, but I was interested in a literary vehicle, and we worked together on the venture."

As it happened, the writing that Betty Owens did in college was a prelude to a career grounded, in large part, upon her superb skill in written communication. It is noteworthy that writing—of the highest quality—has been a key part of the effort called for in all of the positions Betty Owens has held. Oddly, she cannot point to a particular teacher, course, or institution that is responsible for helping her to develop superior writing ability. Whether this talent grew out of the discipline and drudgery of the boring, traditional classes at the Latin School or was a by-product of her extensive reading, she cannot say.

The youngest of eight brothers and sisters, Betty Owens says that everyone in her immediate family was a reader. Today she spends leisure time tending an apartment full of plants and watches hockey games and a few other television offerings. But reading is still a favored pastime—not best-sellers, but a wide range of literary works. Preferred authors come and go. For a time, Virginia Woolf was high on her list; more recently, she has been reading Joan Didion. "I have about three hundred books in my own library," she says. "I enjoy re-reading them too." She likes modern mysteries. Chuckling, she comments, "That is how I keep up with the latest fads, with what is happening in the world."

Betty Owens is a retiring person who cherishes privacy. She doesn't drive (she depends on public transportation for commuting from her suburban apartment to Cambridge), and she is not a joiner. She belongs to no church, no clubs, and no political or social groups. "I guess I belong to the Boston and Massachusetts Bar Associations," she admits, "because that is required." Associates attest that she avoids meetings and social events whenever possible, and that she always shuns the limelight. When the twenty-fifth anniversary of the ITP was celebrated at a gala reunion dinner in May 1977, Dean Albert Sachs of the Harvard Law School lauded Betty Owens. She wasn't there to hear his kind words.

Colleagues weren't surprised. They had seen her "sneaking out" after the cocktail hour.

In one-to-one encounters, Betty Owens is warm, confident, and obliging. She is cordial to visitors and a good friend to the many colleagues with whom she has shared the joys and pains of massive scholarly projects over the years. She spends many off-duty hours with her family—an extensive network of nieces, nephews, and other relatives scattered throughout greater Boston.

One of Betty Owens' biggest fans is her secretary, Rosalin Aronson. Ms. Aronson is a former teacher and also, after hours, a student. She is working to earn a master's degree in psychology. "She has helped me so much," says Ms. Aronson. "Now I am getting A's in my courses—I never could before." It is a puzzling comment, and Ms. Aronson hastens to explain. "I used to be a dreamer," she says, testifying that Betty Owens' habit of working so *steadily* all day long has been an invaluable example to her.

It is clear, even to the casual observer, that Ms. Aronson makes a telling point. Betty Owens is a worker, not a dreamer. The rungs of her own ladder of success seem, pretty clearly, to have been put together with a combination of work and talent. Nor was there ever, one can guess, any danger of her falling off by gazing upward. She states, in fact, that she has never had any grandiose career plans or any fixed, long-range goals.

Betty Owens does confess that she always expected to be a careerwoman. What was her family's reaction? She describes her parents as neutral in the matter, but says that her three older sisters were very supportive of this goal. (Her eldest sister was a certified public accountant who had a distinguished career in the service of the U.S. government in a number of foreign countries.) In talking of her plan for a career, Betty Owens reminisces about the atmosphere of the late 1930s when she made this decision. "In those days," she says, "most of the top female students planned careers. I would certainly say that this was true of the upper quarter of my class at Smith College." She comments on the change— or the "shift backwards," as she terms it—in the decades immediately following. "I was surprised," she says, "that ten or fifteen years later . . . the women of my nieces' generation were intent on getting married and raising families at very early ages."

What was it that ultimately pulled Betty Owens toward a legal career? She can't identify a person or an event. The decision was rather an outgrowth of a variety of experiences that came with her years of government employment in Washington, D.C. After a year of postgraduate study at the University of Chicago, she decided to stop and work for a year before going on to get her Ph.D. in Economics. One year was stretched to seven; one job expanded to four. Initially, she was involved in the early stages of the work of organizing the huge price control administration—an agency that would, during all of the years of World War II, dispense ration coupons and directives of every sort to citizens in all parts of the nation. Her next position, at the State Department, required economic analyses in connection with the presentation of the reciprocal trade agreements to Congress. From there, she moved to help with the work of the United Nations Relief & Rehabilitation Administration (UNRRA), developing procedures for the vast shipments of goods that were made by that agency. For three years, she worked in the Fiscal Division of the Bureau of the Budget.

Why so many changes? She recalls that in the U.S. government offices of the 1940s, there was either an enormous amount of work to be done or virtually none. When the "sitting back" stage came, Betty Owens moved on, looking for new challenges.

Hired as an economist, she admits that much of her government work also involved management and organizational matters. "All of it," she laughs, "brought a great deal of contact with the lawyers." However, it was not exactly awe of the profession that led her to apply for admission to Yale Law School in 1948. "Frankly," she says, "I was more irritated than impressed by the lawyers." She recalls that the lawyers were always called upon to draft materials. "I felt," she says, "that I was perfectly capable of writing anything that had to be written. They (the lawyers) always seemed to think if anyone was going to use the English language, they were going to be the ones to do it." So Betty Owens decided to join them, to get the magic credentials herself.

There were other considerations in her decision to study law—a bit of boredom with Washington and some interest in law from a social science viewpoint. "I have never thought of myself as a reformer," she hastens to point out, "but I was interested to see what role law was playing in society, as compared to economics, for example." She smiles at this noble aim, and says, "As it turns out, of course, once you get to law school, those kinds of questions never occur to you again."

In law school, she discovered that her work experiences were helpful. She also found that her economics training was a very good background for law. What does she recommend as a major to pre-law students today? First off, she says, it is important for lawyers to know the fundamentals of expository writing and to develop unusually good writing skills. She laments the fate of the student who doesn't have "the vaguest notion of how to distinguish the important from the unimportant in developing a written paper on any subject."

She says that poor writing is an indication that there is "something wrong in the way one is thinking." She does not recommend any particular major for pre-law studies because she feels that being a lawyer means many different things. There is practically no college major, she says, that wouldn't be appropriate. She notes, for example, that a number of the students in the natural resources seminar that she teaches have studied the physical sciences. She concludes by saying that she is most likely to advise a pre-law student to "major in whatever interests you sufficiently so you will put a lot of *work* into it." She observes that many young people seem to be surprised at the amount of effort that is required to become really adept in one's chosen field.

Professor Elizabeth Owens is, by any standard, a hard worker; it is also clear that she does not waste much time in getting at the work at hand. Her work schedule has varied over the years, from forty-five hours a week upwards. A "night person," she says she gets going gradually during the day. She is not fond of early-morning classes. Usually at her desk by 9 A.M., she often works straight through the day, skipping lunch if a task is especially urgent. She seldom stays at her office beyond 6:30 P.M. However, a briefcase frequently goes home with her. There may be student papers or journals to read in the evening.

How does she keep up with all of the pounds of books, magazines, and other materials that are delivered to her office each day. "I am," she says, "an efficiency expert in my mind. I never put anything in it that isn't essential; if there is any area in which I am any good, it is in having a keen perception of what I need to know."

Betty Owens' confidence in her professional abilities is well intact and has been for many years. She says that she did not worry during the time she was attending Yale Law

School about finding a job when she was graduated. With that event in prospect in 1951, she began to make the rounds of the Boston law firms. She recalls a number of depressing fifteen-minute interviews. "It was clear that they were not going to hire me," she says. "They just wanted to salve their consciences. I am sure many saw me just so that they could say that they had talked to a woman prospect." These sham interviews were, she says, "extremely infuriating."

When asked if she has often been discriminated against on account of her sex, Betty Owens replies "yes" with no hesitation. She has not, however, been active in women's rights (or any other) movement. At one time, she taught the Harvard Law School course on "Women and the Law," which dealt with discrimination in employment and related issues. She found it interesting but overly time-consuming because it was so far afield from taxes and the other subjects she customarily teaches.

Betty Owens is appreciative of the progress made in the past few years in eliminating discrimination as it relates to women generally, and to women lawyers in particular. Does she think discrimination will vanish? She doesn't reply directly to the question. Instead, she makes two observations. She feels strongly that women still have to work harder than men to achieve the same goals. Further, she believes that the credibility of women remains as a very serious issue. "The authority with which the words coming out of a woman's mouth are treated is a major problem," she says. In many cases, she adds, it is probably not a conscious attitude on the part of listeners. Yet she finds that it is pervasive, obvious in social as well as professional encounters. "The quality of attention given to a man's conversation is quite different," she notes.

Betty Owens feels that her own credibility is in pretty

good shape at the professional level because she has worked hard to establish it. "But this is something many men start out with," she says. She feels that, even in the case of a young man just out of law school, he may be listened to, whereas a young female graduate will still have to demonstrate her capability to establish the same credibility." She recognizes that today a female law graduate may be able to do this in a shorter time—especially in certain settings—but it must be done.

Betty Owens recalls that many female law graduates of the 1950s were offered jobs as legal secretaries. It didn't happen in her case. "Probably the best advice I ever got," she confides, "was from a psychology professor at Smith who was interested in my advancement. She told me, 'Don't ever learn to type' . . . and I didn't."

When Betty Owens' 1951 job hunt reached the Boston firm of Hill, Barlow, Goodale & Adams, she had a different reception. The interview brought an offer. She isn't sure just why, but she notes that it was at that time one of Boston's "Yale" firms. Also, another woman lawyer was already working there, although she was not a partner. (Betty Owens explains that there were no women partners in any major Boston law firm until the 1970s.)

Betty Owens counts her experience at the Hill, Barlow firm as interesting and valuable. Private practice, she says, has the advantage of offering more contact with people. The disadvantage, she feels, is that adequate direction is not always offered to associates. She thinks the expectation that young lawyers will learn what they need to know by a kind of process of osmosis is not always realistic. She recalls being asked to review a contract and finding about two hundred ambiguities and difficulties in it.

When she recounted them in a subsequent meeting with the

client, he was appalled and indicated that if business was
carried on that way, it would grind to a halt. "I had over-
analyzed it," she says. On the other hand, she recalls the
satisfaction of working with a senior partner on a very difficult case that was before the Supreme Court of Massachusetts. It involved the "Rule Against Perpetuities," an ancient
and complex property law that many attorneys don't wrestle
with in a lifetime of practice. Nonetheless, she says, she began to have doubts about her future with the firm when
"they hinted that I take a job with the bank downstairs."

At about this time, Peter Summers, a fellow associate at
the firm, left to work for Stanley Surrey at the ITP. When another opening developed in 1956, Betty Owens joined the
ITP staff. Over the years, she moved from research assistant
to research associate, to editor of publications, and finally,
in 1964, to Director of Research.

The ITP was founded in 1952—a direct response to a
Resolution of the Fiscal Commission of the United Nations
that was adopted on May 16, 1951. In that Resolution, the
Commission acknowledged the importance of trade and tax
policies to the economic development of member countries,
recognized that Harvard University Law School maintained
a center for international law, and requested the Secretary
General to take steps to launch a permanent program for research and dissemination of information concerning tax and
fiscal matters with an international scope. Originally funded
in large part by the Ford Foundation, ITP has also received
major support in recent years from corporations, and law and
accounting firms with an interest in international tax matters.

For some years now, the ITP offices have been located in
the Roscoe Pound Building, which is part of the Harvard
Law School complex. In the early days, the ITP was head-
quartered in the Kendall House at Harvard. A 1958 photo

on display at the twenty-fifth anniversary celebration shows
some twenty-nine staff members smiling from the porches
and balconies on the front of the old house on the Harvard
campus.

Over the years, the staff at ITP has worked in three areas—
research, publication, and the training of tax and fiscal
specialists. In twenty-five years, the ITP produced some
sixty publications. One of the earliest undertakings was the
World Tax Series—a project involving the compilation, in
separate volumes, of the tax and fiscal laws of individual
countries. The twelfth volume, *Taxation in Switzerland*, was
published in 1976. Similar volumes, published previously
deal with such laws in Australia, Brazil, Colombia, France
Germany, India, Italy, Mexico, Sweden, the United King
dom, and the United States. Other publications cover a wide
range of special topics.

Over the years, Betty Owens has edited many of the most
significant ITP publications. Colleagues who know some
thing of the scope of her appraisals protest that the term
"editor" says too little about her role. They note that her input
was invaluable and often extensive; her review of material
frequently led to major changes and improvements. She re
flects that her contribution varied, depending upon her
knowledge of the subject matter. But she admits that, even
in less familiar areas, "I have a pretty good structural sense
of how things should be written, and a sense of whether
something has been missed."

Twice, she was involved in the preparation of massive
bibliographies published by ITP in 1968 and 1975. The 1975
bibliography, co-authored with Gretchen Hovemeyer, con
tains twenty-two hundred references to English language
materials on the international aspect of U.S. federal income

taxation—the taxation of foreign income, foreign taxpayers, and tax treaties.

In recent years, Betty Owens has worked extensively with members of outside firms who help write material published by the ITP. An enormous amount of effort went into a two-volume study, which she co-authored with Gerald T. Ball, a partner in the international accounting firm of Arthur Andersen. Titled *The Indirect Credit,* the huge books deal with the laws and rules involved in transactions involving foreign entities and the interests of U.S. corporations and individual shareholders. Volume I was published in 1975; Volume II is scheduled for publication in 1978. (As noted above, Betty Owens is the sole author of the authoritative 1961 publication, *The Foreign Tax Credit.*)

Presently, Professor Owens is working on a casebook on "International Aspects of U.S. Income Taxation" with William Gifford, a former student who teaches at the Cornell University Law School. The casebook is an outgrowth of materials prepared for law school courses related to this subject, which she has been teaching for several years.

Since 1972, Betty Owens has functioned both as Professor in the Harvard Law School and as Director of Research for the International Tax Program. Some years, her time has been divided equally between the two responsibilities on a straight fifty-fifty basis. In the 1977–78 term, she spent one-third of her time fulfilling her duties as the Research Director at ITP and two-thirds of the time meeting teaching responsibilities. In addition to offerings related to international tax law, Professor Owens now teaches water law and natural resources law.

Unlike so many of today's lawyers, Betty Owens spends a surprisingly small amount of time on the telephone or in meetings. The bulk of her time is spent in study, in conferences with students, and in preparing for classes. She sees students for a variety of reasons. At almost any time, at least one or two students are employed by her for special research assignments. For an hourly rate, students may do "cite-checking" (verifying references for accuracy) or work on more demanding tasks. She confers too with third-year students who must prepare major papers. They come in to submit outlines (required for the papers she will review) and to discuss their proposals. If problems develop with sources more conferences may be necessary. "The amount of time spent with students," says Professor Owens, "is as much or as little as they desire."

Betty Owens maintains a cordial relationship with students, and she has been particularly interested in the women in the Harvard Law School. She reminds the visitor that Harvard—unlike most other United States law schools—has admitted women only since 1950. Betty Owens says that during her initial contacts with the women enrolled at Harvard, she was surprised at their demeanor in the Law School classes. "They were discouraging to me," she says, "I was concerned because they seemed so meek and unassertive. I felt they had a responsibility to *act* . . . and they were just sitting there." She feels that although they were very bright, many of them were unduly intimidated by the competition. "What was especially infuriating," she says, "was to have a girl in class who didn't open her mouth all term . . . and then wrote an A examination paper." Professor Owens regarded this phenomenon as an alarming retrogression because she remembered that the women in her law classes at Yale had been far more outspoken. "I think that perhaps we were at the end of a generation with a wholly different outlook," she concludes.

Professor Owens mentions another intriguing phenomenon that she has observed in watching young women in the professional world over the years. "Frequently, there is a pronounced *gap* in women's devotion to their careers," she says. She notes that she has seen it most often in young women in their twenties, and she muses about whether there may be a biological basis for it. Whatever the reason, she notes that even a short period of waning enthusiasm can be a handicap in a competitive world where substantial and consistent efforts are necessary to achieve ambitious career goals. "Successful women," she says, "are mostly those who have found that they like their work so well that they put in an extraordinary amount of effort."

Betty Owens has been happier listening to female law students in the past few years. They are much more willing to speak out and to assume leadership roles in the law school community. She is delighted that a woman in one of the water law classes she taught recently was an editor of the *Harvard Environmental Law Review,* a relatively new Law School publication.

About twenty-five third-year students were enrolled in that particular water law class, for which Professor Owens used a standard casebook supplemented with mimeographed materials. Minutes before the final session of that term, Professor Owens walked into the classroom and carefully arranged these and other materials on the desk before her. At front and center, she placed the opened casebook; at the right, the mimeo material and a cup of coffee; at her left, a thick folder containing her detailed notes. During class, she sat with hands clasped on the desk in front of her, posing questions to students on a somewhat systematic basis, with few pauses for volunteers. The federal Water Pollution Act of 1972 was under discussion, and Professor Owens made

some comments on the economic issues involved in enforce
ment of this kind of law. Occasionally, a smile softened some
of her crisp remarks, lighting briefly her rounded face with
its frame of neatly trimmed, graying hair, near white at the
crown, darker at the ends.

Now and again during the session, she reached forward
to pick up the casebook to read a passage. Regularly, she
turned to her left to flip a page of the notes she had prepared
for this class meeting. Since this was the final session of the
term, Professor Owens closed by wishing the students well
on their examinations. Afterwards, she gathered the materials
quickly and, in seconds, was out into the hallway. A stocky
figure, Betty Owens walks rapidly, just a hint of a bounce in
each step, her body tilted, the head slightly forward as if
symbolically, it were the leader and anxious to arrive first.

At the elevator, Professor Owens shifted the stack of ma
terials. The thick folder of class notes she always carries
represents long hours of work on her part—and a good bit of
the time of Ms. Aronson's, who types the many pages used
for each day's session from lengthy longhand outlines pre
pared by Professor Owens. Class preparation occupies a siz
able block of Betty Owens' time. She says that if she is
teaching a three-hour course that is new to her, preparation
may consume as much as three and a half days of a work
week, or perhaps 60 percent of her time. The next time
around, preparation time may be cut by half, or more. But
the class notes, with additions, will be on hand for each class
meeting. A disciplined scholar, she moves more or less
methodically through class materials during each term, cov
ering a substantial amount of ground in each session.

Stanley Surrey, who worked with Betty Owens for many
years, describes her as a person whose "incisive mind" forces
others to "think deeply" about any matter that is under con

ideration. In 1961, during the Kennedy Administration, Surey was appointed to a key position in the U.S. Treasury Department. For ten months, during 1963–64, Professor Owens went to Washington too. Taking leave from ITP, she erved as consultant to the Special Assistant for International 'ax Affairs. She played a vital role in the drafting of Model articles for use in the negotiation of income tax treaties. Not ond of the nation's capital, she was glad to return to Cambridge, but she feels that the Treasury Department work was ery useful to her. She had asked for the assignment and it roved to be an invaluable experience. It was not a surrising outcome for a woman with a keen instinct for knowing what one needs to know" . . . and for one who night be called an "intellectual efficiency expert."

HARRIET FLEISCHL PILPEL

Counsel to Planned Parenthood; Practicing Lawyer; Copyright Authority

"I worry," says Harriet Pilpel, "about everything." It is hard to believe. Relaxed, she chats about her work as counsel to some of the leading literary and entertainment figures of the United States, about the benchmarks in the battles of Planned Parenthood, and about her role in the long fight for reproductive freedom for women. Mother, wife, partner for more than thirty years in a prestigious New York law firm and situated in a corner office with a panoramic view of midtown Manhattan, Harriet Pilpel seems to be sitting on top of the legal world.

Leo Rosen, fellow partner with Mrs. Pilpel in Greenbaum Wolff & Ernst, reflects on her genius in making a place for herself as a respected practitioner in a profession almost hostile to women in decades past. She has done so, according to Rosen, because she has a combination of talents that rare in lawyers of either sex—a brilliant mind *and* an infinite capacity for taking pains. The incongruous worry, it seems, is a key part of Harriet Pilpel's success story.

Rosen describes her as a perfectionist. She takes the greatest care with each detail in any legal undertaking, he says, and she assesses every imaginable challenge and weighs the full range of solutions and strategies. It appears that this flair for considering all possibilities is a part of Harriet Pilpel's style. Rosen laughs, recalling an observation made by Ben Kaplan, a Massachusetts judge and a former member of the firm. He told about Harriet's preparation for an autumn weekend visit to Boston. It seems she arrived with bags laden with complete changes of clothing for every temperature from forty below zero to eighty above.

Rosen and Kaplan were among the host of friends and associates who braved the cold on January 7, 1977, to applaud and sing, and to cheer Harriet for the unique honor that came to her that night. The occasion was the annual "Twelfth Night" party at the 44th Street House of the Association of the Bar of the City of New York, and the guest of honor was Harriet Fleischl Pilpel, Esq. Kaplan served as "Master of Revels" for the gala event and fellow lawyers staged an elaborate tribute titled, "Portia Faces Life."

There was dancing afterwards and much hilarity. The atmosphere was in sharp contrast to that of decades past when female attorneys did not tread upon the carpets of this exclusive sanctuary. The Association of the Bar of the City of New York is long on prestige, and honors bestowed by the Association are coveted. The tribute was particularly treasured by Harriet Pilpel who was the first woman to be so honored. As a long-time New York lawyer, she remembered the days when women were barred and the stated reason— lack of proper plumbing facilities.

No such problems threatened at the Ernst firm when Harriet Pilpel began to work there after her graduation from Columbia Law School, or at any time thereafter. As it happened, she joined the firm as an associate at about the same time as Leo Rosen, and both were made partners at about the same time, less than a decade later. This sex-blind professional acceptance reflected the views of the firm's forward-looking senior partners.

Morris Ernst, who died in 1976 at the age of eighty-eight, was, during most of his years at the Bar, a lawyer some steps ahead of his time. A founder of the American Civil Liberties Union, Ernst was a premier fighter for the rights of the individual long before the phrase "civil rights" was in the news headlines. Instigator, strategist, and, often, a field soldier in crucial court battles, Ernst was also a tireless scholar, laboring to mold both legal and lay opinions to shapes more consistent with the social equities as he saw them. From the perspective of a now crowded, expertly trained field, the victories that Ernst won in those days with so few troops seem astonishing.

In landmark cases and lesser disputes, Ernst fought censorship and helped to stake out ever wider perimeters of freedom for the press. He authored and co-authored countless articles and a score of books, including many authoritative works on the issue of censorship in the United States. As an undergraduate at Vassar College, Harriet Pilpel read Ernst's work and cited it in a major paper she prepared on the subject then.

Some years later, when Harriet Pilpel heard Ernst speak to the students at the Columbia University Law School, she was even more impressed. Long before her graduation, she began to think about seeking a job with his firm. "Many lawyers came to speak to the student body," she recalls. "Mostly, they told us that the pathway to success in the law was to make good grades, work hard—that sort of thing." Ernst, it seems, took a different tack, and Mrs. Pilpel was enchanted by his candor. She recalls that he told the students that the surest way to success as a lawyer was to have a lot of money; next best was to marry a lot of money; and, if neither of those routes was feasible, to join the best clubs to make the most helpful contacts.

Whether Ernst was right or those who touted grades, Harriet Pilpel would have no concerns, for her scholarship record was superb—from grade school through law school. She had top marks at Columbia University, where she earned two degrees—an M.A. in International Relations and Public Law and an LL.B. from the Law School, where she was a Kent Scholar and an editor of the *Law Review*. At Vassar, she majored in history and English and was initiated into Phi Beta Kappa in her junior year.

What does she recommend to students today as a pre-law major? She offers no prescription, believing that students should pursue subjects that interest them. She does remember that she took two law-related courses as an undergraduate—constitutional law and international law—which she found to be very helpful. She suggests that students take such courses, not so much for substantive content as to give them a feel for the methodology of the law.

Mrs. Pilpel also counts her debate experience as invaluable. At a very early age, she distinguished herself by winning a Theodore Roosevelt award for an oration on conservation. This experience, she confesses, spurred her interest in public speaking. She was captain of the debate squads at both Evander Childs High School in New York and at Vassar.

Nowadays, she is much in demand as a speaker, often making three or more major speeches a week.

Asked what or who was responsible for her developing an interest in law, Harriet Pilpel, the sophisticated New York lawyer, gives a surprising answer. She says much of the credit goes to "Elsie Dinsmore, a woman who never existed and was not herself a lawyer." Elsie is the heroine of a series of books for juveniles that Harriet read as a child; the lawyers in the stories are her father and her husband. Mrs. Pilpel also recalls that an uncle of hers, who was the wealthiest member of the family, was a lawyer.

She cannot pinpoint the exact time when she made the decision to study law. "I must have been talking about it as a teenager," she says, laughing, "because the caption under my picture in my high school yearbook reads, 'A Budding Portia.'" It is unlikely that the line was in error, for Harriet Fleischl was editor of the yearbook.

Although she was extremely close to her father, young Harriet Fleischl was not a tomboy. She remembers well that she loved dolls, and that she probably played with them longer than most girls. But she also recalls quite clearly that at a very early age, she decided to be a career woman. Both her father and her mother strongly encouraged her in plans for a career. Although the family was not wealthy, all three of the Fleischl daughters were well-educated. All have had distinguished careers.

Ethel Loewy Fleischl, Harriet's mother, had been a teacher. She gave up her career for her family, but not, it appears, without some regret. Today, Harriet Pilpel muses that her long-time devotion to work for women's "reproductive freedom" may well stem from early impressions of this female burden as conveyed by her homebound mother.

In 1933, Harriet Fleischl married New York lawyer, Rob

ert Cecil Pilpel. It is perhaps not wholly coincidental that the females in the Pilpel family were also career-minded. Her three sisters-in-law were career women, and her mother-in-law was a founder of the Child Study Association, an organization devoted to the improvement of the quality of life for children. Harriet Pilpel credits her husband with having a strong influence in the final choice she made concerning her career. In retrospect, she says she is certain that she would have had a career under any circumstances, but if she had married someone who was not a lawyer, then perhaps the law career would not have been so easy to choose.

Twelve women were graduated in her Columbia Law School class of 267 in 1936. As one of the few female students in the law school in the 1930s, was she concerned about finding a job on graduation? "Perhaps at first," she says, "but after I made the *Law Review*, no." She reports that it was then "well-known" that if you wrote and edited the *Law Review*, job opportunities would be more readily available. Interestingly, this still remains true today.

Although Harriet Pilpel wrote and edited the *Law Review* and ranked second in her class, she was in for a few surprises when she began seeking employment. As a top student, she was eligible for a clerkship to a judge. As it happened, the New York judge to whom she was referred was a bachelor. He wanted no part of a female law clerk. Furthermore, he told her that he felt that "a woman's place was in the home." The phrase may have been trite, but it blocked that doorway all the same.

From there, Mrs. Pilpel took her resume to a Wall Street firm. Looking at it, the interviewing partner said, "It's such a tragedy!" Harriet was momentarily puzzled. The "tragedy," he soon explained, was simply that the applicant was a *woman*. "If you were a man," said the chagrined partner,

"I'd hire you on the spot." There was a hint of a job, however, in the firm's estate and trust department. Taken to the dismal, secluded stacks to meet the other two women in this department, Harriet shuddered and made a quick, never-to-be-regretted decision that this kind of work was not for her.

Mrs. Pilpel had always hoped to work for the Ernst firm, but early in her last year of law school, she had a severe jolt concerning employment opportunities with that firm. The word at the school office was that the Ernst firm would not be hiring anyone that season. When she confided her disappointment to her husband, he advised her to ignore that and go to the firm herself. To this day, she makes plain her gratitude to her husband for this sound advice. She talked with Morris Ernst. The interview was a smashing success and the job seemed assured. Later, of course, she worried about whether Ernst would change his mind.

She was attracted by Ernst's forthright manner. Moreover she knew of the interest of Ernst and the firm in civil liberties work. The interest paralleled her own, and she has, over the years, devoted a huge share of her time to such concerns. She has also been deeply involved in other facets of the law. Today, as one of the members of the executive committee of the firm, she also plays a key role in influencing the direction of the firm's activities. She estimates that about 60 percent of her own work involves the literary and entertainment field. The balance is in the field of law relating to sex, marriage, divorce, birth control, abortion, and women's and children's rights.

Harriet Pilpel has served on advisory panels to the U.S. Copyright office, and she is author and co-author of numerous publications concerning her special fields of activity. To her office come requests for rights, and contracts connected with the publication, or possible infringement, of works of prolific writers like the late Edna Ferber and other well-known authors. Scores of her clients are drawn from her network of contacts in the creative establishment. It is scarcely surprising that she finds that more than half of her time is devoted to representing clients in the literary and entertainment worlds.

It is significant that the other 40 percent of Harriet Pilpel's work is in the sex and family law area—another highly people-oriented specialty within the legal profession. Of the total time that Mrs. Pilpel spends in this area, perhaps 10 to 15 percent involves dealing with divorce or other domestic problems. The rest of this work is in the very specialized area of family planning and the law. The firm is general counsel for Planned Parenthood at the national, international, and local (New York) levels. Other lawyers in the firm now handle such matters as taxes and insurance, but Harriet Pilpel handles most of the substantive matters for the vast Planned Parenthood superstructure.

As legal advisor to Planned Parenthood, she has, for years been a captain of the legal ship. She has been in the center of the turbulent battles over the marketing of contraceptives and the dispensation of family planning advice. She was in the forefront of the advocates pressing for the removal of legal barriers to abortion and to family planning assistance. She is proud of her role in making such help more widely available to American women. Asked to describe the legal issue closest to her heart, she does not hesitate. "Other freedoms for women," she says, "have little meaning without reproductive freedom.'"

Harriet Pilpel has argued two cases before the U.S. Supreme Court—one from each of the branches of law in which she has labored for so many years. One was a libel action. The other case was one involving the constitutionality of a Connecticut statute barring the use of contraceptives.

Was she tense as she stepped up to argue before the nation's highest court? Harriet Pilpel had, of course, helped to prepare briefs in other U.S. Supreme Court cases. On several previous occasions, she had been present in the Court as an understudy when cases were argued by Morris Ernst or Edward Greenbaum. Nonetheless, she admits that when the time for argument drew near, she was "scared"—until she got up to speak. The Justices, who had appeared to be exceedingly bored and weary, "seemed to wake up on hearing a woman's voice," she says, "and this gave me a tremendous boost." She laughs and says that perhaps this is one place where her *sex* was in her favor, not through any wiles on her part, but simply because a female voice was different. Having heard the Justices question lawyers in other cases, she admits that she was terrified of the late Justice Frankfurter. She was pleasantly surprised when he turned out to be most considerate in his questioning.

These occasions were, clearly, among the many high points in Harriet Pilpel's distinguished career. Through both the "highs" and the "lows," her husband has been a tremendous support. Mrs. Pilpel counts this as a most important factor in her success in managing to pursue her career while raising a family. The fact that females in *his* family were career oriented was clearly a plus. "I think," says Mrs. Pilpel, "that my husband would have thought it peculiar if I had not had a career."

Her children, Robert Harry, a Yale Law School graduate who is now a successful writer, and Judith Ethel Appelbaum, an author, managing editor of *Publishers Weekly*, wife, and mother, are now grown and are achievers in their own right.

But Mrs. Pilpel frankly admits that the years of their growing up were challenging ones for her.

Did she anticipate the problems in maintaining both career and home? "Not really," she says. "I always knew that I wanted to have children, and I was equally determined to have a career. With a smile, she adds, "I was hoping to do it all—perfectly."

It didn't work out that way. The children thrived, the career prospered, but perfection—by her standards—seemed to elude her, and she was distressed. She recalls that she wanted to plan the birthday parties, shop for the children—to do all these things. Meantime, her stature and her responsibilities in the professional world were growing. She fulfilled both maternal and professional obligations. But when she could not do everything, she was troubled. "In the early days," she says, "I was consumed with guilt because I found that I just could not do everything as well as I wanted to." Adjustments were necessary, she confesses. "But it was some years before I was comfortable about it." During this era, she wrote of her feelings, and how she coped, in an article that she recalls having titled, "The Technique of Compromise."

From a wholly different vantage point, her son remembers these years and says candidly, "If anything, my mother did too much for us." He says that as children, he and his sister were far from neglected. "I think," he says flatly, "that we were a bit spoiled." He notes that, as a child, he was seldom called upon to do domestic chores. "If asked to help," he says, "I usually sulked and complained." A bachelor now, he contends that when he has children, he will assign them definite tasks. Describing his mother as "extremely conscientious," he says that he thinks she went out of her way "to do things for us that we were capable of doing ourselves."

A graduate of Stanford University, where he earned B.A. degree with Great Distinction in history, Robert di not practice after graduation from Yale Law School. Afte a four-year stint in the U.S. Air Force, he followed his "rest less urge to write." The author of *Churchill in America: A Affectionate Portrait* and other books, he now lives an writes in Rome. Judith, the mother of two lively youn children, lives and works in New York. After working fo Harper & Row, she was Senior Editor of *Harper's Magazin* and Managing Editor of *Harper's Weekly*; she is now Man aging Editor of *Publishers Weekly*. Her husband, Alan Ap pelbaum, is a partner in a prestigious Wall Street law firm and their two children, Lynn and Alec, are a source c never-ending pleasure and gratification for Mrs. Pilpel. O a table in her office, there are pictures of the grandchildrer and she looks forward to the hours she spends with ther just about every Saturday in Connecticut (where Alan an Judy also have a "retreat" a few miles away from the Pilpels Both of Mrs. Pilpel's children remain close to their parent:

According to Mrs. Pilpel, neither of her children, whe they were young, ever expressed any resentment about he role as a working mother. Robert theorizes that they ac cepted the situation because it was the only one they ha known.

During the years of child rearing and career buildin; Mrs. Pilpel kept an arduous schedule. When the childre were small, there was a live-in nurse; in later years, hel came in during the day. In any case, Mrs. Pilpel recalls tha she spent about two hours with the children each mornin; getting them set for the day, before leaving for the office.

"For about fifteen years," she says, "I voluntarily reduce my compensation on account of my presumed lesser co: tribution to the firm." She notes that other women at tl firm later followed this pattern. Was it a fair solution? Looking back, she says, "I am not sure if I would do it again. I probably worked just as hard and probably deserved full compensation."

Harriet Pilpel recalls that she did not use day care outside the home. She notes that the common illnesses of children are a problem and often complicate such arrangements. Of course, helpers in the home often disappointed her too. Relatives were seldom called upon to baby-sit, but her husband was sometimes able to fill in at home. For many years now, the same housekeeper has been with the Pilpels. However, Mrs. Pilpel says that even when good help is available, there are many tasks that cannot be done by others. Shopping for home furnishings and attending school functions are duties she remembers well.

Under any of the arrangements made, Mrs. Pilpel's days were long when the children were young and sleep was sometimes disturbed. How was it possible to keep going? Mrs. Pilpel believes that having a tremendous amount of energy was (and is) vitally important to career-minded mothers.

Harriet Pilpel is not a "hustler," but she exudes energy. An attractive woman, she dresses more conservatively, often in soft browns or blues, than many of her clients. She talks at a measured pace in a beautifully modulated voice that brings pleasure, even to the ears of adversaries. Evidence—very convincing evidence—of her sharp mind colors the conversation on any topic. The determination shows too. The listener is left with no doubt that, given an assignment, Harriet Pilpel would complete it—with skill and imagination; that given a challenge, she would meet it—squarely and with vigor.

She was presented with a unique challenge some years

ago when a doctor prescribed, as a substitute for ineffective medicines, a walk of at least two miles a day. Her first reaction was astonishment at the suggestion. "I've no time in my schedule," she protested. Typically, she found a creative solution. For almost a decade now, she has walked to work each morning—a two-and-a-half-mile hike that takes a precious forty-five minutes each day. She has converted it to a special time. "It is my thinking time," she says. "I review cases in my mind, think about people to be contacted, chores to be done. I am amazed at the number of matters that I am able to work out during my hike each morning."

Those at the law firm who work for Mrs. Pilpel can testify to the truth of her comment. When she arrives at the office each morning, she brings a long list of items for follow-up. Although they readily admit that they hustle all day to keep up with her, the women all describe Harriet Pilpel as a "fantastic person." Theoretically their responsibilities are carefully divided, but they help each other out when emergencies arise. In the fast-paced-world of Harriet Pilpel, this is often.

Ruth Kogan, who is Mrs. Pilpel's Administrative Assistant, and who handles all the stenographic work, says that on most days it is a very heavy load. For the past few years Mrs. Pilpel has made use of a dictating machine connected to a telephone that has a special number, so that she can telephone her dictation directly to the office from anywhere in the world at any time, for Mrs. Kogan to transcribe. The volume of work is such that Ruth is ably assisted by two other very competent women who also work for others in the office but help Ruth with the phone calls, file checking, routine correspondence, and other tasks.

When Harriet Pilpel is in town, Ms. Kogan finds waiting

on her desk each morning to be transcribed many memos and letters that Mrs. Pilpel has dictated at the end of the previous working day—reflecting all items that have been handled during that day and indicating what needs to be done and who is to do it on each matter. There are crises from time to time, but Mrs. Kogan finds the work with her talented boss to be stimulating.

Full briefcases go home with Harriet Pilpel each night. Colleagues estimate that she carries home from "fifteen to twenty pounds of work" each night. They laugh about it, but few doubt that the scales would support their guesses. Asked how she does this volume of work after a full day at the office, Mrs. Pilpel smiles. "I do some work on week nights, but most is saved for weekends. It is necessary to carry some of it home each night, however, because I couldn't possibly lug it all with me on Friday."

What is in these briefcases, some of them so well-used that the papers poke through frayed, open seams at the corners? The first is that client matters are kept in separate briefcases. A good deal of the other material is reading matter—journals and advance sheets that keep her up to date with the latest happenings on the diverse legal fronts in which she operates. There are also a host of notices, reports, and background material related to her committee assignments.

Over the years, Harriet Pilpel's extracurricular activities have been varied and almost beyond number. A partial list of such commitments in a recent edition of *Who's Who* included: Counsel to Special Committee on Divorce and Marriage Laws of the National Conference of Commissioners on Uniform State Laws; Past member, Board of Directors of Planned Parenthood; Member, Advisory Board of

Arthur and Elizabeth Schlesinger Library on History of Women in America; Counsel to Sex Information And Education Council of the United States (SIECUS); Member, Committee on Political and Civil Rights of the Commission on the Status of Women appointed by President John Kennedy; Member, special task force on status of women of Citizens Advisory Commission appointed by President Lyndon Johnson; Member, Board of Visitors of Columbia Law School; Member, Committee on Law, Social Action and Urban Affairs of the American Jewish Congress; Vice Chairperson of the National Advisory Council of the American Civil Liberties Union and Chairperson of the Communications Media Committee.

She is also a member of assorted bar associations at both local and national levels, of the American Academy of Matrimonial Lawyers, and is a member and former trustee of the Copyright Society of the U.S.

In 1973, Harriet Pilpel received a special award from SIECUS, and in 1974, she was given the Margaret Sanger award for distinguished service to Planned Parenthood. Both honors came for her work in effecting changes in law that made sex education and family planning services available to more Americans.

Harriet Pilpel has never shunned controversy. As a staunch defender of women's right to reproductive freedom, she hailed the 1973 decision of the U.S. Supreme Court that held unconstitutional state laws that barred abortion in the first trimester of pregnancy. Some months later, she appeared on national television on William Buckley's program, "Firing Line," to make a spirited and articulate defense of the Court's position. She has also appeared on many other television programs discussing a variety of questions arising out of her special interests.

Each month, Harriet Pilpel has many speaking engagements. The groups that solicit her services at the podium vary widely. In a recent year, she made a major speech at the American Library Association Convention. In 1973, she was honored to be asked to deliver the Bowker Memorial Lecture at Columbia University Law School. Her speech, titled, "Obscenity and the Constitution," was later published in booklet form for wider distribution. As a rule, she accepts only invitations to speak about subjects she knows very well —those which will not require time-consuming special preparation. However, when she senses that she might be getting stale, she will try a new topic.

She has written articles and books on many themes related to her fields of specialization, several with co-authors. She has written frequently for *Publishers Weekly*, for some years doing a column entitled, "You Can Do That?" Of all the materials she has written, she says that she is proudest of the now-outdated volume, *Your Marriage And The Law*, which she wrote with New York attorney Theodora Zavin.

Despite the overflowing schedule of professional commitments, Harriet Pilpel does have some social life. Dinners and theater parties occupy occasional evenings. However, a good share of her weekends now—winter and summer—are spent outside of the city at the Pilpel's Connecticut property. The setting is decidedly rural, and the quarters for the Pilpels are in an old barn, painstakingly remodeled over a period of many years.

On such weekends, there are five-mile hikes to the village and cozy evenings in the rustic shelter. Despite the diversions of the surroundings—the lure of the natural splendor—Harriet Pilpel finds hours each day for the never-ending work. The life-long habit tells much about her energy and her determination, perhaps even more about her abiding interest in certain areas of the law. These enthusiasms have taken Harriet Pilpel to the topmost regions of the legal system, and they doubtless account too for her youthful posture of looking zestfully to the future.

LOUISE BALLERSTEDT RAGGIO

Family Law Authority; Reformer; Private Practitioner; Bar Leader

"Attending night law school was the cheapest thing I could do to get out of the house," says Louise Raggio. She recalls that the cost was about eight dollars a semester when she began attending night classes at Southern Methodist University (SMU) Law School in the late 1940s. Cooped up with two toddlers, in shabby postwar housing set in a sea of Dallas mud, car-less and without funds for sitters, Louise Raggio says—without smiling—that she had to escape to preserve her sanity. Her husband Grier, Sr., a lawyer then working for a meager salary at the local Veterans Administration offices, was available to baby-sit in the evenings. "In fact," she confides, "it was his idea. I had not thought about studying law." It is an incredible admission, coming, as it does, from a woman who is nationally recognized in her profession, and the recipient of a host of local laurels as well.

The escapee-housewife fleeing each night—sometimes on a bicycle—to the quiet halls of the old law school in the basement of the "Old Main" building on the SMU campus seems a far cry from the successful practitioner who sits behind the broad desk in the elegant offices of Raggio & Raggio today. At her back is a view of the city where she made it happen, the ever-changing skyline of downtown Dallas, visible above a row of lush plants crowding the sill of the huge window. On the adjacent office walls are rows of plaques and citations that represent only some of the honors that have been bestowed upon Louise Raggio.

On the shelf beside her desk is a copy of the new Texas Family Code. It represents what may be the crowning achievement in her distinguished career. The new set of statutes, a major revision, is the accumulation of a decade or more of effort spearheaded by the diminutive Dallas lawyer. Long years in the family law practice had convinced Mrs. Raggio of the need for revisions. As Chairman and an active member of the Family Law Section of the state Bar, she pushed hard for adoption of the changes. She marshalled task forces for drafting, and people to explain the reforms to groups across the huge state. Doggedly, over several years, she lobbied to move the crucial measures through often balky legislatures. When the job was done, she reviewed the Texas "story" in the American Bar Association's (ABA) *Family Law Quarterly*, sharing insights with the many lawyer-readers who were seeking similar reforms in other states. In 1975–76, she took time out to chair the prestigious Section on Family Law of the ABA.

Louise Raggio shares another special joy with only a very few of the thousands of lawyers that practice in the United States today. She has three sons who are lawyers, and all are active in the profession. The eldest, Grier, Jr., practices in New York City. The other boys, Tom and Kenny, practice in Dallas as members of the Raggio firm along with Louise

Grier, Sr., and two other partners. Both parents claim that they did not push the boys to study law. But both are clearly pleased that their sons have chosen to pursue legal careers. Grier, Jr., received his undergraduate degree from Harvard and his law degree from Boston College. Tom and Kenny are University of Texas men.

Grier, Jr., was born in 1943, Tom in 1946, and Kenny in 1949. During the years that Louise was enrolled in law school (from 1947 to 1952), family responsibilities loomed large. The demands upon her time were ceaseless. She recalls that her last year at SMU Law School was especially hard. In the early years she had taken courses on a hit-or-miss basis with little guidance. "I suppose everyone thought I would just drop out after a while," she says. That final year, she was forced to attend some classes in the daytime and some at night to meet the requirements for graduation. Did she ever have doubts, in those difficult times, about whether she was doing the right thing? "Probably every day," she replies without a smile.

Kenny's own law school application years later must have startled the admissions officers. On it, he wrote, "I think it is only fair to tell you that this is my second time through law school. . . ." Louise testifies that Kenny first attended law school at the age of nine months. Born during Louise's five-year stint at SMU Law School, Kenny was often in the basket of her bicycle as she pedaled to school. On arrival, he sometimes went with her to class. More often, he sat in a corner of the library. In those more informal days, Louise recalls, the librarian would sometimes help keep an eye on him. As he grew older, she brought crayons and paper to keep him occupied.

Louise's classmates, who were mostly veterans with young families themselves, were sympathetic and helpful. Within a short time, many fellow students became "buddies" (Mrs. Raggio's term for male associates with whom she developed a special rapport). Always a large group, it has expanded over the years to include a good share of all of the male colleagues with whom Louise has ever worked or served on committees. Few women were then enrolled in the SMU Law School, but one friend, in the class ahead, was Barbara Culver, who later became a judge in west Texas. Both Louise and Barbara were pregnant at the same time, and the Culver child was sometimes a companion for Kenny at the law school. Louise says she appreciated the favorable climate in which Kenny was received, but she readily admits that the real key to her success in taking Kenny to school was that he was a remarkably good boy. She confesses that she would have had no such luck in bringing her middle son who was known, in those days, as "Tommy the terror." She says he would have torn the place apart.

Mrs. Raggio was further weighed down in law school years by a steady stream of scoldings from her mother, who advised her that she was going to "ruin" the children. "My father may have thought I had lost my marbles," says Louise, "but he did not say anything. Mother piled guilt after guilt upon me." Louise confesses that it was a heavy burden, but she believes it may have strengthened her resolve. "I think it made me so mad, I just stuck harder."

Whatever she thought of her daughter as a mother, it is unlikely that Hilma Ballerstedt had any doubts about Louise's academic ability. From the first, Louise was a superior student. Raised on a dirt farm in south central Texas, Louise journeyed to Austin High School and was graduated at the top of her class at age sixteen. At the University of Texas, she was an honor student, named to Phi Beta Kappa in her junior year.

As an undergraduate, she worked to obtain a teaching certificate. She recalls that in those depression years, it was vital to study something that would lead to a job. Would she take the same courses again? Emphatically not. She muses that, without such economic concerns, she might well have majored in geology or astronomy—subjects that still fascinate her. She mourns about the time spent in the education departments. "I wasted twenty-six semester hours on extremely dull courses. I wish I had taken interesting electives instead."

She is grateful that she was able to enroll in some journalism classes, and that she found time to work on the newspapers in both high school and college. What does she recommend to students today as a pre-law major? She feels that any discipline that makes the student think is useful. The development of good writing skills, she says, is "absolutely essential" for lawyers. She also urges would-be lawyers to study Latin and to take accounting courses.

After graduation from college, Louise received a Rockefeller fellowship for graduate work in public administration at American University in Washington, D.C., and she was an intern with the National Institute of Public Affairs for a year. It was a mind-stretching experience. Participants were a select group of thirty students—twenty men and ten women —from across the country. Several members of the group— James MacGregor Burns and Harlan Cleveland, among others—later gained fame, distinguishing themselves in a variety of interesting positions.

Participants in the Institute program attended lectures by government leaders and spent time at a number of government agencies. There were many memorable treats. Not long after Louise and her group came to Washington, Eleanor Roosevelt invited them to the White House for an informal supper. "She was very cordial," says Louise, "chatting with each of us. I remember being impressed by her kindness in putting at ease a young man who was painfully embarrassed by a gaffe."

Asked how this unique honor came her way, Louise says that, one day, just by chance she happened to see a notice about the program on the bulletin board in one of the buildings at the University of Texas, and she decided to apply. Why was she chosen? She shrugs and modestly observes that "they probably were looking for someone from this part of the country."

Louise Raggio's story about the bulletin board notice and her follow-up tells much about her style, alert to opportunities and willing to invest·time in pursuing them. Her husband, Grier, Sr., says of her: "Louise is a very ambitious person. She is always looking for ways to utilize her time more efficiently." He says, too, that she has a very rare combination of firmness and sensitivity. Grier Raggio, Sr., makes no effort to hide his admiration for his wife. "She is the best *human being*—male or female—that I have ever known." He admits, however, that he was first drawn to her by her intellectual ability. They met when both were working for different government agencies in a remote area of south Texas. Already a lawyer with considerable experience, he recalls that she was the first literate person he had met in months. "She was like an oasis in the sagebrush," he says with a laugh.

They were married a few months later, in April 1941. On December 5, 1941, just hours before the news of Pearl Harbor, Louise found out that she was pregnant. When Grier, Sr., went overseas for military duty she went back to the farm. She and Grier, Jr., spent unhappy war years with her parents. As she tells it, she was literally "stuck in the mud" of rural Texas. Many of the roads were unpaved. When it rained, they were impassable.

Mrs. Raggio did manage to get to Austin often enough to assume an active role in the League of Women Voters and, in 1945, she served as president of the group there. Contacts with her school friends in the area were renewed and strengthened during this period too. Louise's associates note that, over the years, she has developed a vast network of friends throughout Texas. Considering the staggering demands made on her time by chores at work and at home, it is hard to imagine how she found time to nurture so many personal relationships. But there is no question that Louise Raggio did, and does, treasure friendships. "In time of trouble," says her colleague Reba Rasor, "Louise is the first one there with the hot dish." Friends who are hospitalized get personal notes. For many years, Mrs. Raggio was active in the Unitarian Church. A church publication titled "One Hundred Outstanding Women" honors Louise Raggio, in company with Clara Barton, Louisa May Alcott, and ninety-seven other notables.

Reba Rasor, now a partner in Raggio & Raggio, is the wife of Dallas attorney Mac Roy Rasor, a friend of Louise's from grade-school days. A former journalist and society editor of the Austin *Herald-Statesman,* Reba attended law school later in life, after her children were in school. Louise was a constant source of encouragement to her. Mrs. Rasor says she is far from alone in this. Louise, she says, constantly bolsters friends, and sometimes clients, in innumerable ways.

In landing her first legal job, Louise was herself the beneficiary of support from another woman, Dallas judge, Sarah Hughes. Judge Hughes has been on the bench for forty-two years—twenty-six years as a state judge and sixteen years in the federal court. She was in the national spotlight in 1963 when she was summoned by Lyndon Johnson to administer the Presidential oath to him aboard Air Force One at the time President Kennedy was assassinated. Over the years, Judge Hughes has been extremely active in pressing for the placement of women lawyers on the bench and in other key positions. So it was that, in 1954, she called friend Henry Wade, then local District Attorney. "As I recall," she says, "I simply suggested that he appoint Louise Raggio to his staff."

Mrs. Raggio says that when she began work as an Assistant District Attorney, she was the only woman among the twenty-six assistants. She says that the men, including Mr. Wade, were pleasant, but "probably figured I would fall flat on my face." She adds, "After I had been there about a year, Mr. Wade admitted to me that it had been easier to hire me than to have Sarah Hughes on his neck." Long before that, however, he and others in the office had come to appreciate Louise's talents.

Louise Raggio faced a challenging task in those early months. She was assigned to handle a number of juvenile law matters that no one had been doing much of anything about for years. She recalls that files of cases needing attention were stacked three-feet-deep on the floor. Texas had adopted the Uniform Reciprocal Enforcement of Support Act in 1952, but the bulk of the hundreds of inquiries from other states had not been answered. Within a month, Louise prepared forms. She says that they were done in haste and were not exemplary, but they were used in the office for some years thereafter.

Within a few months, the men in the District Attorney's office were her "buddies." She says that when they found out she didn't ask for any favors and didn't cringe over details of any cases, they accepted her. Sometimes, she recalls, they asked her to prosecute certain cases. "Let's face it," she says, "I can be a lot rougher on a woman witness or defendant than a man can." She was the first woman to serve as a prosecutor in the criminal court in Dallas. When Texas opened jury service to women in 1954, she was the first lawyer to try a case before an all-woman jury.

As an Assistant District Attorney, Louise spent arduous hours in the office each day and, very often, she brought work home to do at night after the children were in bed. Nowadays, she is less likely to bring briefcases home, but she often goes to the office on Saturdays or Sundays. Do professional women still have to work harder than men? She nods and adds that she believes that this will be true "in the foreseeable future." She feels that for some years there will be prejudice, though perhaps at the subconscious level. She points out that the older men who are in charge in law firms and elsewhere come from backgrounds that still influence their thinking. Will the women of her sons' generation fare better? "That depends," she says, "on the mommas and the papas they have had."

Mrs. Raggio recalls that when she was graduated from law school, the placement office refused to take her application for employment, indicating there were no opportunities for her and suggesting it would be "kinder" not to mislead her. She also recalls that the men who were Assistant District Attorneys were making more money than she was. But she says, "As discriminated against as I have been, I can't remember ever getting worked up about it."

Louise Raggio flatly denies setting any grandiose career goals for herself. The man with the plan, it seems, was her husband. He confirms the story that it was his idea for Louise to go to law school. To get out of the house? Yes. But he adds that he also saw this as a way of extricating himself from the government service where he was unhappy. Both he and Louise, he says, were "kids of the depression." He had been self-supporting since age sixteen. With no extra funds, or any important connections, he knew that establishing a practice would be difficult. Louise's talent would help.

In the early 1950s, the plan came to fruition. When the job at the District Attorney's office materialized, Louise was delighted. "Grier, Sr., was getting more and more anxious to quit the federal government, and I knew I had to have a paycheck." The following year, he opened the law office in Dallas. As it happened, it was not long before Louise quit her job to join him as partner in the firm. Both had been worried, but the firm prospered from the start.

"To our surprise," he says, "we were able to make it from that first month." Louise's work had generated a lot of interest. Also, she developed special skill in the juvenile and family law fields while in the District Attorney's office. Her practice developed along these lines. Today, she handles a number of estate and probate matters, but the bulk of her efforts are in the domestic relations area. Now one of the leading lawyers in Dallas, she has handled divorces and property settlements for some of the city's wealthiest and most prominent families. She represents men as well as women. However, she feels her special talent lies in helping women whose husbands have left them after twenty or thirty years of marriage. It's a familiar scene—wealthy older man anxious to marry winsome younger woman; abandoned wife distraught. Louise knows how to hang tough until her clients are able to secure fair settlements. She says that such arrangements often take a great deal of patience—some involve negotiations that take months, or even years. Frequently, Louise Raggio spends many additional hours counseling her clients, encouraging them to look at life as a new beginning rather than a sad ending. "If I am good at anything," she says, "it is in working with women who are about my age."

A superb speaker, Louise Raggio is frequently asked to address groups on the subject of "Women's Legal Rights." It is a topic on which she can be eloquent. Her genius lies in being able to reduce complex legal doctrine to simple terms, easily understood by laypersons. As one listener observed, "When she talks to women at a club meeting about what will happen to them if their husbands die tomorrow, without a will . . . nobody naps."

Louise Raggio's reputation appears to rest upon a thorough knowledge of the laws and an extremely practical approach in applying them. Her pragmatic bent is apparent in her reflections about formal training in the law. She feels that "law school was, in many ways, a waste of time because so much of it was theoretical." Chuckling, she says that, in her view, the correct answer to some of the examination questions would be "to tell the client to forget about it."

Louise Raggio is, at the same time, a dedicated pursuer of the ideal. She will doubtless be long remembered for her monumental contribution to reform of the Texas family law. Knowledgeable Texas lawyers credit her as the key figure in the long fight that finally brought the revised Family Code to the state. Her ability to appreciate both the ideal and the practical is apparent in an insightful passage from the recital of the Texas saga in the ABA's *Family Law Quarterly*. Written with colleague Reba Rasor, the article was aptly titled "From Dream to Reality . . . How to Get a New Code on the Books." In it, there is this telling comment:

When one raises the banner of reform, one attracts idealistic, reform-minded persons who . . . are welcome. But it is also important to search out and bring in some good old-fashioned, hard-nosed reactionaries, some instinctive and, if possible, vociferous opposers of the new and different. They may . . . arouse homicidal urges in other group members, but they also prevent mistakes and keep enthusiasm within practical bounds.

In the article, readers are advised how goals were achieved, step by step. There is information about the task forces composed of lawyers and legal scholars that met to draft and debate provisions, and about the lawyers who spoke to both Bar and lay groups throughout the state to build the public support that influenced lawmakers to vote for the proposed reforms.

In the 1965 session of the Texas legislature, revisions eliminating discrimination against women in the management of community property were passed. In 1969, the legislators were induced to make major changes in the law of marriage and divorce, including the addition of a form of "no-fault" divorce which is now used in 90 percent of the divorce proceedings in the state. In 1973, parent and child provisions were revised, as well as the statutes related to the juvenile court and the Texas Youth Council.

Over the years, Louise Raggio was often called upon to testify before the legislative committees. Along with professional lobbyists of the Texas Bar Association and others, she also kept track of the progress of the various bills. Looking back, she shudders. "Lobbying," she says, "is a zoo." She laughs recalling that her persistence was not always appreciated. During the energy crisis of 1973, she recalls that one exasperated legislator told her, "You don't have to worry . . . you can fly anywhere on your broomstick."

The chances are good that he later chuckled over the com

nent with her. Louise Raggio has the ability to develop
rapport with friend and adversary alike. For years, she has
moved most of the hours of each day in a man's world. Small
in stature, with now-graying hair simply fashioned, somewhat indifferent to style, Louise Raggio does not present an
imposing appearance. But her voice is compelling, her
warmth inviting—camaraderie comes easily. Whether she is
walking in the mixed crowds on the Dallas streets, or moving
through the buffet line in the posh City Club in the new sky-
scraper floors above, Louise Raggio smiles and returns
greetings from friends and acquaintances in almost nonstop
sequence.

Louise Raggio is a popular figure in Dallas, but her reputation extends far beyond its borders. She confesses that she
has contributed thousands of hours to voluntary service. In
1970, she won the Zonta award "in honor of her outstanding
leadership, vision and ability, and with appreciation of her
distinguished and unselfish service to the state of Texas and
Dallas County." In 1974, she received a special award from
the Business and Professional Women of Dallas for going
the "extra mile" for law reform.

Another significant honor came to Mrs. Raggio in Mon-
treal, Canada, in August 1975 when she accepted the gavel
as Chairperson of the five-thousand-member Family Law
Section of the ABA. It meant, of course, an enormous amount
of work. Each day brought a suitcase full of mail, and the
assignment reduced her practice time by half. Nonetheless,
accession to the post signified that Louise Raggio had earned
the respect of the most successful lawyers in her field. It was,
in a sense, a supreme tribute.

No one disputes that Louise Raggio deserved these
honors or that she has made generous gifts of her time. The

only question, in most minds, is *how* she was able to do so—
and at the same time meet her obligations in her own home.

One of the secrets, quite obviously, is her enormous
energy. An early riser, she and Grier, Sr., are usually in the
office well before 7 A.M. and they often leave after 5:30 P.M.
They prefer to miss the rush-hour traffic for the drive north
to their home in University Park, just blocks from the SMU
campus. They moved to this area in 1949 to ease Louise's
commuting difficulties and they have lived here, in two different houses, ever since.

Arriving before the office is humming, Louise usually turns
on the machine to dictate replies to letters, motions, briefs,
or directions regarding other matters. "In a couple of hours
each morning," she says, "I can generate enough work to
keep the staff busy for the rest of the day." Her secretary
Suzanna Griggs, confirms this observation. She describes her
job as a "high pressure" one.

Over the years of her practice, Louise's hours at the office
have always been long and strenuous. Because of the nature
of her practice, trips to the courtrooms for motions, hearings
or formal trials are often on her daily calendar. For most of
these years, she has come home each night to prepare dinner and, very often, go out again to attend a meeting or
speak to a group.

Grier, Sr., has always been supportive. Louise is proud of
the boys and asserts that they too were very helpful. She is
critical of mothers who do everything for their children, and
she feels that they cripple the children by not allowing them
to develop self-reliance. She feels that driving kids every
where is a poor practice. "My kids," she says, "learned to use
their legs and their bikes." This apparently worked fairly well
because schools and most activities were close by. Kenny

recalls one difficult time. "In ninth grade," he says, "it was not 'cool' to ride bicycles, so I had to try to get rides or walk a lot."

When Louise joined her husband in the firm, they both knew that the hours she would have to spend downtown would be long and difficult. They held a family meeting, according to Louise, and discussed the sharing of the work. The boys' memories (they were then twelve, eight, and five) are a bit hazy on this point, but Tom recalls that it was often his job to set the table. It was the boys' chore too to wash the dishes. They recall fighting about "turns," and their joy when they moved to the house with a dishwasher.

For a short time, Louise employed a woman who could pick up Kenny at school and be in the home until Louise arrived from work. For the most part, the only paid helpers in the Raggio household have been there for once-a-week cleaning. Louise does recall that no matter how busy she was, she made it a practice to spend a little time alone with each boy every day. She has no use for those who do not meet such parental obligations. "These days," she says, "you have a choice about whether to have a child. When you give birth, you have a responsibility. I don't believe a person should have a child and then just pack the child off to a day-care center all day, every day."

Louise has always done most of the cooking in the Raggio household. It is a task that neither her husband nor the boys enjoy, though all have some capability in the kitchen. Kenny, a bachelor for some years, confesses that he prefers eating out or fixing snack-type meals. What about grocery shopping? the laundry? other mundane chores? Kenny praises his mother's efficiency. "She did most of it," he confesses.

Tom is married and a father now. He baby-sits some evenings each week while his wife works. Her former employer has pressured her to come back to work full time. Tom says that he is not enthusiastic about the prospect of having to do any more at home. "Like my father," he says, "I don't mind baby-sitting, but I dislike housework."

Over the years, Grier, Sr., put in countless hours baby-sitting with the boys in the evenings. Early on, he developed a creative solution to the problem of getting them to go to bed. He had the boys race around the block each evening until they were exhausted and ready for sleep.

The boys credit their father's exercise program for their subsequent success in track. Both Tom and Kenny were varsity lettermen in track in high school. All of the boys were involved in other activities too. Tom and Grier, Jr., were Eagle Scouts. Grier, Jr., was president of the student council in high school; Kenny, a representative. All played on Little League and other neighborhood teams. Grier, Sr., and Louise were often there when the boys competed. Tom estimates that his mother was on hand to cheer for at least 75 percent of his scheduled games.

Tom also remembers his mischief and when he went through a period of rebelliousness that was hard on his parents. The summer he was fifteen, he and a friend decided to hitchhike to Florida. Instead of forbidding it, Louise and Grier, Sr., gave him a note that said: "To whom it may concern: Our son, Thomas Raggio, is in process of traveling to Florida and has our permission to do so." The note was valuable; it brought release three times when the boys were picked up by police. The trip also proved a valuable lesson for Tom, whose behavior improved considerably after that.

Louise freely admits that raising three lively boys was a strain at times. A serious eye injury kept Tom in the hospital or thirty days—with Louise beside him, day and night. Louise also recalls leaving the office a few times when there were crisis calls from the boys. She says she trained the boys not to disturb her at the office over minor matters, but she made it clear that she was there if she was really needed. Mostly, it appears, the boys managed nicely on their own in the hours after school. They remember well that they had the first color television set in the neighborhood.

The boys don't remember much concern about the fact that their mother worked, unlike most other mothers in the neighborhood at that time. Kenny says that once, in an argument, a friend taunted him about it. The boy, a neighbor, remembered the incident. "Years later," says Kenny, "he apologized for it." Tom recalls that for a while when he was in elementary school, he was a little uneasy about his mother working. For a time, he says, it seemed a stigma to him.

Louise was (and still is) acutely aware of the critical community atmosphere of the 1950s. She talks about her own response, her efforts to be a "supermom." Louise Raggio participated, it seems, in the full gamut of expected parental roles. At school, she supplied endless cookies, was a room mother, and even helped to serve school lunches. At the elementary school the boys attended, the cafeteria detail was assumed by mothers. Louise bent her work schedule to perform this inconvenient chore. At one point, she was forced to explain to District Attorney Wade why she had to be gone on certain lunchtimes. Looking back, she says, "It was ridiculous. But it was important to the boys that I *be there* dishing up the ice cream like the other mothers, so I went."

"Being there"—when the men in her family have needed her—has consumed vast quantities of energy and hours. When one reflects on these totals, and the magnitude of her other contributions, Louise Raggio's feat in establishing a lucrative local legal practice and a state and national reputation in her field seems more than spectacular, and very near to impossible.

PATRICIA SCOTT SCHROEDER

Political Activist; Congresswoman from Colorado

United States Representative Patricia Schroeder has often called herself a "troublemaker." Although she selects it herself, it is not the best word to describe the tall young brunette who serves as congressional spokesperson for a majority of the citizens of Denver, Colorado. Elected to her third term in 1976, Ms. Schroeder has been making waves for some years as one of the most articulate liberals in Washington, D.C. It is true that the "waves" have brought troubles—sometimes to the chairmen of the committees on which she serves and, often, to the more conservative members of the House of Representatives. But the waves aren't those of a helmsman up to mischief, or of a motorboat out of control. The waves, if they come, may be due to speed and an unwillingness to slow down for traditional shoals, or to accommodate to pressure for less noise, or to accept guidance from pilots more experienced in navigating the murky congressional waters.

Courageous and knowledgeable, Pat Schroeder is a formid
able advocate for the reduction of U.S. military spending and
other positions she believes in. She can claim, too, another
strong advantage in going about her work in Washing
ton's political thicket. She has a refreshingly independent
attitude about her position on the Hill. Not yearning for a
life-long tenure, she says that she can afford to speak out
without concern for reprisal. She feels that she is in a better
position to shun deals and trade-offs than members of Con
gress who have more ambitious goals.

"I was happy," she says, "with my law practice in Denver
I enjoyed my other work—teaching in a number of the col
leges in the Denver area and serving, part-time, as a hearing
officer for the state of Colorado. And I had plenty to do at
home, caring for two small children." It is easy to believe
Pat Schroeder when she says she did not seek the nomination
for the congressional seat and won't weep when and if her
Washington duties draw to a close.

None of this means that Pat Schroeder takes her responsi
bilities lightly. Serious in both her goals and in her day-to-
day demeanor, Congresswoman Schroeder has committed
herself to an unbelievably demanding schedule. It is clear
that Pat Schroeder is a person who understands full well the
harvest that hard work yields. Now in her upper thirties, she
confesses that she has had this particular insight for a very
long time.

"I got my first job when I was fourteen years old," she
says, "and I worked during most of my years in high school."
Was the family in need of funds? She shakes her head. "No,"
she says, "but my father believed strongly in the value of
work experiences for young people. He also encouraged my
brother and me to be as independent as possible."

Congresswoman Schroeder describes her upbringing as

unusual." Thoughtfully, she tells the visitor that she was raised "somewhat differently from most young people of my generation." It seems that there was, on the one hand, a strong encouragement for her to work, a heavy parental push toward the practical. On the other hand, there were lots of privileges. Rules and restrictions were light in the Scott household. The emphasis, for Pat and her brother, was on self-discipline.

Pat Schroeder recalls that she took flying lessons at an early age and secured her pilot's license when she was only seventeen years old. "My brother and I also had the use of cars when we were quite young," she recalls. "And there were no rigid edicts about where we went and when we would be home. It was left to us to use good sense," she says. Her father was in the airplane insurance business and there was almost always a plane for family use. Unlike most families, the Scotts used their own plane for many family vacations. In the late 1940s and early 1950s, there were exciting trips to Cuba, Alaska, and other destinations.

A hard-headed businessman, Lee Scott is visibly proud of his daughter. "I wanted my kids to understand the practical side of life at an early age," he says. He feels that many young people don't get such insights until they are well into adulthood—too late, in many cases, to alter the life patterns they have established. He believes that it is most important for young people to learn not to waste time—a belief that his daughter, quite obviously, shares.

Lee Scott says that Pat was always a self-starter and a hard worker, at school and elsewhere. He describes her as a person who learned, when she was quite young, to stick with a job until it was completed. He points out that she also had to learn not to be too dependent upon friends and associates because the Schroeder family moved several times during her school years. Her mother worried about the effect of the moves on Pat and her brother. But her father saw this nomadic experience as useful in that it taught the children to adapt to new situations and to get along with all kinds of people. They learned to make their way with strangers, he says, because they were not able to stick with the same group of childhood pals as so many young people do.

Her father acknowledges that it wasn't always easy for Pat to "make her way" in the new settings. She was cross-eyed as a little girl and wore thick glasses until she was an adolescent. Looking back, Pat Schroeder says that school was not the main focus of her life during her high school years, as it is with many young people. Lee Scott's gentle nudge of his daughter into the working world also reduced the time she had for school activities.

Pat Schroeder's outside commitments did not, however, affect her academic performance. She finished near the top of her class in high school. At the University of Minnesota she majored in history and philosophy and, in 1961, she was graduated from that institution *magna cum laude*. It was a considerable honor, made even more impressive because she had completed four years of work in three years, not including summers.

When did she decide to study law? Did her parents approve? She recalls that her parents were pleased and very supportive. She says that she cannot pinpoint the time when the decision was made. There was no "bolt from the blue"—no memorable moment when her career was revealed to her in a lightning flash. She recalls thinking about a legal career during high school days. Later, as an undergraduate at the University of Minnesota, she weighed both law and medicine. Law won out, as she remembers it, simply because with each passing term, her commitments in the social

tudies department seemed to grow at a faster rate. Applica-
ions to law schools were made, and the fall of 1961 found
ier enrolled at the Law School of Harvard University. Why
Iarvard? "We talked about it," says Lee Scott, "and I said
o her that since she was a woman and would face stiff com-
ietition, she would be better off with a degree from a law
chool with a fine national reputation." The freshman class
t Harvard Law School that year contained few female stu-
lents. Less than a dozen women were graduated with Pat
chroeder in the class of 1964.

During law school, she anticipated that she might have
lifficulty finding a job as a lawyer following her graduation.
ihe was not mistaken. She recalls clearly that, during inter-
iews, she was asked the same question that had exasperated
nd annoyed female law graduates for decades . . . "Can
ou type?"

Discriminatory attitudes were prevalent and, in those pre-
ffirmative action days, little effort was made to conceal
hem. She recalls being told by a representative of a well-
nown Chicago firm, at the very outset of one interview, that
here was no possibility that she would receive a job offer
rom that firm. The interviewer frankly confided to her that
ie would not be talking to her except for the rule of the
Iarvard placement office that prohibited him from inter-
iewing other prospects if appointments made with women
nd minority students were cancelled.

Pat Schroeder's job search was complicated by another
actor. In 1962, she had married James White Schroeder, a
ellow law student at Harvard. Both were programmed for
raduation in 1964. Seeking jobs in the same cities, there
vere problems about conflicts of interest that might arise.
'at had taken a number of tax courses and hoped to special-
ze in that field. When Jim took a job with a Denver firm,

she inquired about a legal position with the Internal Revenue Service and was told that she could not work in any office closer than Santa Fe, New Mexico.

Once settled in Denver, Pat Schroeder was not idle. She worked as a field attorney for the National Labor Relations Board for a time. Later, she served as a hearing officer for the department of personnel of the state of Colorado. For some years prior to her election to Congress in 1972, she had a law practice in Denver. Most of these years, she was also occupied as a part-time professor in several colleges in the Denver area. She taught at the Community College of Denver and at the University of Denver. For two years, she also conducted classes in the social studies department of the private Regis College in Denver.

During these years, Pat Schroeder's responsibilities at home were growing. Her firstborn, son Scott William, arrived in 1966, and daughter Jamie Christine was born in 1970. In the early days, there was part-time household help at the Schroeders, and invaluable assistance from reliable baby-sitters. In recent years, there has been a full-time housekeeper in the Schroeder home. The children have also spent much time with grandmother Scott in Denver. Bernice Scott, who taught school for many years, loves the role and says, without any qualifying comment, that her grandchildren are her "greatest joy."

Congresswoman Schroeder is appreciative. But she is also candid in commenting that help—whether it comes from family or via employment agencies—is only a *part* of the answer. In accounting for whatever success she has had in combining career and family responsibilities, she names three other vital ingredients: 1) an abundance of energy, 2) a supportive spouse with a sense of humor, and 3) a flexible approach to life-styles. Although Pat Schroeder says she has

een lucky in all of these "essentials," she is frank in sharing
er feelings about the enormity of the task. She is still awed
y the mass of details related to her professional and mater-
al obligations that must, somehow, be woven together into
workable fabric each day. Asked if it is true that she had a
ipply of disposable diapers for infant Jamie in her purse at
er congressional swearing-in ceremony, she nods in the
ffirmative. No laugh or flippant remark follows the cónfes-
on. There is only a sober observation, "There were times in
1ose early days in Washington when I really wondered if I
Duld do it all."

Nonetheless, Pat Schroeder shuns the omnipotent image.
he says, rather, that with small children and a demanding
areer, "Something has to go, you simply cannot go every-
here and do everything." In her case, she says the cuts have
Dme in the Schroeder's social life. "There just isn't time for
1tertaining," she says.

Asked about her favorite sports or recreational activities,
at Schroeder says she has none; that there is no time for
1ch diversions. She also adds that she watches almost no
:levision. She encourages her children to do the same. It is
n approach that may stem from her own parents' attitudes
>ward television viewing by Pat and her brother when they
'ere growing up. "They didn't prohibit it," she says, "but
1ey strongly discouraged us from spending much time in
1is way."

Congresswoman Schroeder's appearance does not give the
nallest hint of her hectic life. She is calm, unharried in man-
er, and very well put together. Staff members stress that she
ncourages them to be informal, to be comfortable, but Pat
chroeder herself presents a trim, polished image. She is
lessed with a model's figure. Seeing her dressed one week-
ay morning in a gray dress of fashionable cut, a chain at the

neckline, a *Vogue* editor would find no fault with the pictur
A squinting of the eyes, from time to time, offers the on
evidence of strain or perhaps fatigue. The strands of her lor
hair shine—clean, hanging loose, but in perfect order—a tid
complement to the oval face with the intent eyes.

The anecdotes that Pat Schroeder freely shares reveal he
present perception of priorities and her maneuverings i
managing her time. She has often confessed to those wh
ask "how she does it all" that she has taken virtually no tim
for shopping in recent years, and that she has ordered unbe
lievable items via the telephone. She may be the first perso
in America to telephone a dealer to order a stationwagor
There was simply no time for browsing—for "tire kicking"
in the showrooms of Denver's auto dealers for the vehic
that was needed for the move to the nation's capital. Sh
also put in a long-distance call to order carpeting for th
Schroeder's new home in suburban Virginia, across the Pot
mac from Washington. In neither case did she worry abou
details such as color. She told the astonished salesmen at th
other end of the wire in each case that she would take wha
they had in stock. The newly elected representative wa
sandwiching domestic tasks in between her congression
chores.

Has she ever had to cancel a professional engagement o
account of homemaking chores? She responds that she ha
not. "If conflicts develop," she says, "I bring the childre
along." On one occasion, she moved eight-year-old Scott
birthday party to the sedate House of Representatives dir
ing room so that she would be able to attend an importan
hearing nearby.

A more widely known example of the children's "visiting
in mother's place of work is the time when she brought the
to the Capitol to help with a "cause." She was pressing har

for passage of a bill for increased federal funding for child-care services. The Schroeder children, along with several other youngsters, were highly visible to those on the floor of the House of Representatives during debate on the measure. She looked upon this as a useful reminder for the older representatives, whose own life-styles shielded them effectively from the practical problems of so many of today's mothers.

As a member of the House Armed Services Committee, Pat Schroeder puts in long hours of study on the hundreds of proposals that come before this key congressional committee each year. A critic of many of these measures, she feels an obligation to be especially well informed. Sometimes, she is at odds with the majority of the members of the Committee. Often, she feels that the congressional leaders may be too timid in responding to the initiatives of the U.S. military establishment.

Because of the huge volume of material to be considered and reviewed, this Committee frequently meets as often as four times a week. Pat Schroeder is there, always prepared to question the spokesman for the proposals and, often, to inquire about alternative plans. An opponent of spending for the B-1 bomber, she was elated with President Carter's announcement in the summer of 1977 that he would not support development of the sophisticated craft.

Because she has so often opposed legislation that increased expenditures for military purposes, she has devoted many extra hours to research and to persuasive efforts to defeat or modify bills at the committee level or on the floor of the House of Representatives. Although she has not served in the military, Pat Schroeder does not hesitate to get into the specifics of Pentagon proposals. She argues generally that the monies appropriated for military purposes would be better spent in people-serving programs such as those administered by the Department of Health, Education and Welfare.

Pat Schroeder vigorously opposed the congressional pay raise voted for by Congress in 1977. She felt it was inflationary. She also pointed out the clear evidence that it was strongly opposed by the electorate. When the measure passed despite her objection, she announced that she would donate her after-tax increment to the Denver Children's Museum.

About once a week, Congresswoman Schroeder attends the meetings of the House Post Office and Civil Service Committee, of which she is a member. She serves as chairperson of the sub-committee on Employee Ethics and Utilization, an assignment that brings an additional round of meetings. Attorney Chuck Knull, who is now counsel to the subcommittee, is a former administrative aide to Congresswoman Schroeder. Like the rest of her staff members, he is a more than enthusiastic Schroeder fan.

Hired during a congressional recess, Knull says that he did not meet Pat Schroeder until about a month after he had begun to work in her office. "I was impressed immediately," he says. "I just knew she would be great to work for." He confesses that he knows many legislative aides (or L.A.s, as he terms them) who don't like working for women. Knull has the opposite feeling. "I think working for a woman has advantages," he says. "I think you have better communication and less pomp." Like other of the Schroeder staff members, Knull loudly professes his hatred of "pomp."

Former aide Kitty Hardy, who worked closely with Congresswoman Schroeder in her Washington office, says that she appreciated the informality of the Schroeder office. Interestingly, Schroeder's aides also characterize themselves as "troublemakers." They are clearly proud to be associated with the congresswoman who so frequently livens up congressional dialogue on the floor or at committee meetings with her penetrating inquiries.

Pat Schroeder's aides describe her as one who remains calm whatever the pressures in the office may be. It seems a bit astonishing, considering the number of items that are on Pat Schroeder's agenda each week. Yet her deliberate manner is consistent with the label. There is no breathless rushing about, but one gets the feeling that things get done in the Schroeder office, and perhaps more efficiently than in many other offices on Capitol Hill.

Knull notes that Representative Schroeder was one of the first members of Congress to shift the bulk of work with constituents' problems to the local (Denver) office. Several other representatives later followed her lead. They adopted this strategy to free their Washington staff people so that they could spend more time on legislative matters. Staff aide Nancy Downs, who has spent time in both the Denver and Washington offices of Congresswoman Schroeder, describes the work as entirely different in the two offices. A University of Colorado graduate, Nancy was an intern in the congresswoman's office in the spring of 1976. She joined the staff in time to handle scheduling and press relations for that year's campaign and has had a variety of assignments since that time.

Knull believes that Congresswoman Schroeder's credibility in the eyes of her constituents has increased very visibly during her tenure. As they have come to know and appreciate her intelligence and her sound management of responsibilities, they have turned to her more often. He recalls that in the early days, local executives attending a conference in the congressional offices often looked to male aides rather than to the congresswoman for replies to the tough questions. "That does not happen anymore," he says. "They have come to respect her."

If constituents' concerns occupy a large block of the congresswoman's time, so do contacts with other members of Congress. Committee meetings are just a small, formalized part of the network of relationships that are tended by all hard-working representatives who occupy the seats of honor on Capitol Hill. For years, Pat Schroeder reserved many Tuesday lunchtimes for meetings of the congressional women's caucus informally chaired by Bella Abzug or Margaret Heckler. Pat Schroeder is a loyal friend of all who labor in support of women's rights. They are never left wondering how she will vote on the key issues that are important to the women's movement.

As a conscientious congresswoman, Pat Schroeder is often "on the road." Twice a month or more often, she flies to Denver to be in touch with constituents and their problems. She must also keep abreast of developments in the busy local office in which ten people are now employed full time. This is about twice the number that keep the Washington office running smoothly.

At times, Jim Schroeder and the children go along with Pat on the weekend trips to Colorado, but travel costs and other activities often keep them in the Washington area. On occasion, Jim and the children attend congressional gatherings. They went along to a well-publicized charity event featuring Republicans versus Democrats, with the members competing in a variety of sports events. A weak contestant, Pat Schroeder won no ribbons, but she did gamely enter both the bike race and the sixty-yard dash. A good sport, but not a great athlete, Pat Schroeder participated because she felt it important that the women in Congress be represented.

Jim Schroeder took a cut in salary to move to a new job with a law firm in Washington, D.C., and he now has a schedule that is a bit more flexible than his wife's. He can be reached for emergency calls from the children's school. Also, he can get home earlier in the evenings to spend time with the children. Pat and Jim are frank in admitting that, just now, her responsibilities as a congresswoman have to take precedence. Both also admit that they don't always expect it to be this way. They have an open-minded view of their marital roles. Both are prepared to shift roles to meet the needs and opportunities that may come their way.

Asked if she thinks that there is still some criticism of the mother who works, Congresswoman Schroeder says "yes" very quickly. She adds, however, that perhaps the criticism now appears in different forms. She herself believes that the quality of time that is spent with children is more important than the quantity of time one is in their company. It is well that she feels this way. After long days on the battlefront in Congress, she brings home about four hours worth of paperwork to do each night at the Schroeder's split-level home in suburban Virginia. She is more than grateful that Jim can be there on the frequent occasions when work keeps her late on Capitol Hill, and she is glad that he can be there with the children on the weekends that she must fly to Denver without them.

If Jim is ever unhappy with any of the arrangements—which he says he isn't—he can only look to himself to blame. He chaired the Democratic committee charged with finding a candidate for the congressional seat that Pat won in 1972. It was he who did the persuading and pushing necessary to get both committee members and his wife to go along with his suggestion that Pat Schroeder be the candidate.

Jim Schroeder had been a candidate himself. He ran for

the Colorado legislature and lost in 1970. But one finds no
trace of envy in his voice as he discusses his wife's achieve
ments. Jim is a cheerleader. He and Pat both believe that
dual careers can work if one partner is willing to play a sec
ondary role sometimes, and if the partners never compete
Any impartial scorer would have to give them an "A" for
their accomplishment in putting that theory into practice.

IRENE FEAGIN SCOTT

Tax Attorney; Judge, United States Tax Court

A visitor to the offices of Judge Irene Scott notices first the blend of colors in the Kerman rug and the tapestry on the wall beyond. The window wall behind the Judge's huge desk, with its view of the Georgetown University Law Center, attracts the visitor's eye too. But not for long. When Judge Scott rises and begin to speak, the background fades. The strong, gravelly voice is compelling, vibrant with the accents of an Alabama youth unaltered in forty years of mingling with Yankees in the capital and in the courtroom outposts of the tax circuit that includes the whole nation.

Judge Scott has been traveling that circuit—handling incredibly complex, million-dollar tax cases—as Judge or a government lawyer, for decades. She recalls her first session as a Judge. It was in New York in June 1960. A host of friends were there. Many had worked with her when she appeared on the other side of that bench as a trial attorney in the Appeals Division of the Chief Counsel's office of the Internal Revenue Service (IRS). Some were colleagues from her days on the Excess Profits Tax Council. Others had known her, more recently, as a Special Assistant to the Chief Counsel at IRS. Now members of the New York tax fraternity, they looked on with satisfaction as Irene Scott assumed her new role as Judge on the sixteen-member U.S. Tax Court.

Some well-wishers were transplanted Alabamans who had come to cheer. The "Southern connection" is an important part of Judge Scott's life. Over the years, she has carefully tended family ties, honoring the old traditions of courtesy and hospitality despite the incredible demands upon her time. For during the era when she sweat to keep ahead of her caseload at the office, she was, at the same time, maintaining a home and raising her children, Tom, Jr., and Irene, Jr., without any visible limitations on the scope of their activities. Today, both young Tom and Irene are themselves lawyers and both are employed in demanding legal positions.

Graduates of prestigious colleges and law schools, the children laud their mother's efforts and seem hard-pressed to name ways in which she shortchanged them. "Looking back," says Tom, Jr., "I think of mother as, if anything, too conscientious. I remember that we had supervision in the household after school all through high school and *long* after my sister and I thought we needed it." Few mothers worked in those days, and Tom, Jr., is aware that, in spite of her efforts, his mother was sometimes criticized. "My mother doesn't suffer in silence," he says, "so we heard about it. But, make no mistake, my mother isn't one to let others run her life either."

Tom, Jr.'s, comments say a lot about the Judge's strengths— but not quite all. Talking with her, the other ingredients of her success as wife, mother, and eminent tax attorney begin to unfold. A primary boost, she readily acknowledges, was the strong encouragement to study law that she received from her own family from the very beginning.

The neatly framed formal photographs of the court that hang on the walls of the Judge's office show that for twelve years (1960–1972), she was the only woman on the court. Two others had served before her—Judge Herron and Annabel Mathews, who was appointed to the predecessor body, the U.S. Board of Tax Appeals, in 1930. Reciting a tale of almost unbelievable coincidence, the Judge tells how she happened to hear of the far-off appointment of Miss Mathews while she was an undergraduate at the University of Alabama.

As a freshman, Irene Feagin was one of three girls honored for earning the highest academic records that year. Called into the office of the president for congratulations, she had revealed to him her longtime plan to study law. The president advised against it. Shaken, she wrote her father. Arthur Feagin replied promptly, encouraging her to stick to her plan and enclosing a newspaper clipping about the Mathews appointment. In the letter, her father wrote an uncannily prophetic message—"I feel quite sure that if you live up to [my advice], you will come out like the woman whose write-up is enclosed."

Sadly, Arthur Feagin did not live to see his daughter appointed to the court. Nor could he, in 1930, possibly have known the course her life would take. But he did know her, and he had great confidence in her ability. What is more remarkable—in the atmosphere of nearly fifty years ago when most women happily (or unhappily) tended the home—is that he encouraged her to study *law*. In those days, women who had any post-high school education were routinely shunted into teaching. Judge Scott says, however, that she would probably have received the same advice from her father in any era. An achiever himself, Arthur Feagin was graduated in 1909 from Auburn University with a degree in civil engineering and the highest academic record made at that institution up to that time. Captain of the Auburn football team, he played under John W. Heisman, the famous coach who inspired one of the most coveted awards in football, the trophy that is awarded each year to the player voted best in the nation by United States sports writers.

Judge Scott's mother, Irene (Peach) Feagin, was equally enthusiastic about Irene's goal, and with good reason. Her own father—a man ahead of his time—had seen to it that each of his ten children, including his daughters, received a college education. Peach Feagin gave up teaching when she married, but she strongly supported her daughter's career plans. A different parental attitude might have hampered the Judge, because the family was not wealthy. There were many times, says the Judge, when it was unclear where the money would be found to educate Irene and her younger sisters.

Arthur Feagin's sudden death in 1932 was a severe shock, and it brought hardship in those depression years. Irene was then a first-year law student and her sister was a college freshman. To earn extra money, Irene had been helping out in the office and library at the law school. When the librarian left, she was offered a full-time position. "The title," she says, "was grander than many of the chores." But it did bring funds, and a plan developed. Irene would work until her sister finished college when she, in turn, would work to help Irene finish the last two years of law school.

In the Feagin family, a plan made was a plan executed. After two years, Irene reentered law school as a second-year student. Does she regret the time lost? Judge Scott booms an emphatic negative. "It was a good thing," she says. "I was a better student the last two years." She hastens to add, "My grades didn't change much; I had had a good record. But, being more mature, I got more out of the material." Few women were then interested in law but, as it happened, five were graduated with Judge Scott's class in 1936.

The Judge says her involvement in tax work was an accident. But her finding a job in Washington, D.C., was not—it was the result of a carefully executed plan. As a female law graduate in 1936, she faced two major obstacles. The first was the bleak employment picture for everyone that year. The second was the bias against female attorneys in most quarters of the legal profession. Exploring local opportunities, she found poor fare. She rejected clerical work in law offices as inappropriate for her training. She was especially determined to avoid this route because a cousin had once derided her decision to enter law school saying, "Go ahead and get a law degree, you will make some lawyer a fine secretary."

Briefly, she considered "hanging out a shingle" in her hometown of Union Springs (Pop. 2,000), or elsewhere in Alabama. But she realized that this would mean a heavy involvement in real estate and family law—fields that were not too appealing to her. The message of the times seemed to be, "Go North, young woman."

In the fall of 1936, she headed for Washington, D.C.—with the plan. She would apply for legal positions at promising agencies, get another job to provide funds to live on, and wait. If nothing happened in a year, she would return to

Alabama. Interested in business law, she concentrated on three agencies—the Federal Communications Commission (FCC), the Securities and Exchange Commission (SEC), and the then Bureau of Internal Revenue (now IRS). Applications were submitted. Doggedly, she followed up in moments when she could slip away from her job as Grade 2 clerk at the Works Progress Administration (WPA). One day she met a former classmate who told her that he had heard that Internal Revenue would be hiring attorneys to help with the new "unjust enrichment" tax. Ecstatic, she hurried to see the personnel chief there. He was discouraging, refusing even to discuss the possibility of her employment.

Undaunted, she visited the Alabama congressional offices and was able to arrange an appointment with the then Chief Counsel of the Bureau. In that office, Irene Feagin made quite a different impression, and on November 2, 1937, she reported for work at the Bureau—beginning a lifetime of wrestling with the toughest tax issues that taxpayers or government officials could create. "Immediately," she says, "I knew that I had found my field." Asked what she would have done if she had felt otherwise, she seems surprised. "Why, I'd have resigned, of course."

Cases come to IRS attorneys when taxpayers challenge the assessment of taxes made against them by government agents. Generally, the law gives unhappy taxpayers two routes for challenge. They can pay the taxes, under protest, and sue for refunds in the federal courts. Or, if they don't wish to pay, they can file petitions with the U.S. Tax Court asking for decisions on the issues they've raised.

The role of attorneys in the Appeals Division, where Judge Scott spent so many years, is to represent the government in Tax Court cases. It means, on the one hand, a lot of hard digging to get the "facts"—reviewing reports, conferring with officials, and assembling evidence to support the government's position. It also means researching the law. In the case of taxes, this includes not only reading court opinions and the tax laws in the Internal Revenue Code, but also checking regulations written to implement the laws and the countless rulings that interpret the statutes and regulations.

"It was hard work," says the Judge, "but very satisfying." She readily admits that she worked very long hours, especially in the early days when so much was unfamiliar. "I suppose, too, that, consciously or not, I did more because I knew that more would be expected of a woman."

From the first, Judge Scott liked the courtroom work, but she describes the task of preparing for trials as "extremely demanding." She doesn't think a good trial lawyer can work a nine-to-five day, at least not during a trial. "When I was trying cases," she says, "I worked many eighteen-hour days. So much must be done outside the courtroom—reviewing and preparing exhibits, talking to witnesses, planning strategies, and drafting questions or motions."

Judge Scott was working such days during the years when her children were very young. In 1939, she had married Thomas Scott, Sr., an engineer and fellow Alabaman, and their children were born in 1943 and 1947. During times when most mothers are spending eighteen-hour days on the home front, Judge Scott was operating at full tilt on the professional stage, building her reputation as a top tax litigator, and somehow meeting her maternal obligations as well.

It is obvious that determination is a key element in the Judge's success. She doesn't recall exactly when she first decided to study law, but it was before high school. "I think," she says, "I was interested in law from the time I could read books and newspapers." She won't call herself a "leader," but she seems to have been an achiever at an early age. At age ten, she was county winner of an oratorical competition sponsored by a Birmingham newspaper. At about the same age, she first met Senator Lister Hill (then an Alabama congressman) when she gave the child's presentation at a Memorial Day celebration in her hometown. Not long afterwards, she and a few friends spurred adults into starting the first Girl Scout program in town.

Judge Scott says that an equally important element in her success in meeting demands of both office and home is the support offered by her husband. Though not disposed to help with housework, Tom, Sr., was always encouraging. "If I had had a husband," she says, "who expected me to greet him at the door each evening fresh as a daisy, it just wouldn't have worked." As it happened, however, Tom, Sr., was overseas with the U.S. Army when the toughest decision came. Taking leave in December 1943, the Judge went home to Alabama to have her first baby, Tom, Jr. "For a brief time," she admits, "I was brainwashed by the intense pressure on mothers to stay home. I thought perhaps I could care for the baby and do some legal work part-time."

But it was not to be. "Instead," she says, "I ended up on the front porch in the afternoons with friends who also had babies and husbands overseas. All they talked about was how terrible it was that we were there without our husbands." "I've never figured it was any use to sit bemoaning what was a fact," she says. The aimless conversations spurred her decision to return to Washington as soon as possible. When she revealed her plan to the local pediatrician, she recalls that she suffered a tongue-lashing in tones so loud that a friend in the outer office offered sympathy when she emerged. Despite the doctor's dire warning—that working full time was the "equivalent of ruining your child's life"—she was unmoved.

Early in March 1944, she went to Washington and located a furnished apartment. Then she returned to Alabama and found a nurse. March 15 found baby, nurse, and mother on the train headed for the capital. Grateful that she had taken leave instead of resigning, she reported for work again on March 17.

Tom, Sr.'s, welcome return from service brought an increase in domestic obligations. The growing family needed larger quarters. Details were endless. She recalls with a laugh that their present home, in which they've lived for twenty-five years, is three feet lower than planned. "I was busy on an important case," she says, "and neither Tom, Sr., nor I were here when they put in the foundation. By the time the error was discovered, it was too late to make a correction—so our lower level is more like a basement."

Judge Scott says that she had good luck, for the most part, in finding help. Housekeepers did not live in, but they were a part of the Scott household for more than twenty years, until Irene, Jr., went off to college. "Just three people," says the Judge, "were with us most of those years." Between those times, there were some rough periods. She can tick off the names of a few people who "didn't work out." "My first priority," she says, "was that they be good with children. The house came second. But there were problems. One woman, whom the children loved, finally had to be dismissed when petty pilfering expanded to the stealing of pillows off the furniture."

"I tried outside day-care," she says, "but it just didn't work for me. I had to get Tom, Jr., fed, dressed, and delivered each morning, and pick him up at a set time." It is too limiting, she feels, for anyone with a demanding job. Travel complicated matters, but even in the Washington office, she says she couldn't always walk out at closing time. "More important," she adds, "when your child is being cared for elsewhere, *nothing* is being done in the home." This means that the mother's job, she says, must be such that it leaves her with the energy to do laundry, cleaning, and other tasks after she gets home in the evening.

The last is a telling comment, coming from the Judge, who freely admits that she is a person with lots of energy. A "night person," she regularly retires at 1 A.M. and is up at 7 A.M. "Even when we are on vacation," she says, "I'm never able to sleep more than six hours." Have the extra two hours a day given her an edge over more sleep-needy humans? Laughing, she confides that she has always counted it a blessing.

Despite her energy, Judge Scott admits there have been plenty of challenges. Mostly, she met obligations head on, armed with assorted strategies. Never lucky enough to have a housekeeper with a driver's license, the Judge solved transport problems for the children in two ways. One, by choosing a home site near a regular bus line. Two, by carefully screening taxi drivers each school season and locating one who could be called in emergency situations to carry a child from school or to special activities.

Recalling her efforts to be a model parent-participant in school and community affairs, the Judge talks of some of the demands. A dutiful P.T.A. officer, she missed lunch on Tuesdays one season to attend 1 P.M. meetings scheduled by the nonworking mothers. As a Girl Scout leader, she was long committed to a nonstop series of regular and special meetings. A Sunday school teacher, she was also, for a time, a Sunday school superintendent at the Methodist Church in

Arlington, which the Scott family has belonged to for many years.

In spite of the contributions, critical remarks from other mothers were not uncommon. She confesses that at times she felt, too, from some of them, the hot breath of envy. But she won't dwell on details. "Mostly, I tried hard to forget who had said what," she concludes. But she does ruefully recall that she could not find much comfort then even in reading the newspapers for, in that era, the big guns of the media fired unceasingly upon the working mother.

There are other gray memories. Both children had reading problems in their early years. Emergencies too tested the Judge's confidence in her chosen life-style. At age two and a half, Tom, Jr., had a ruptured appendix that was not diagnosed correctly until grave peritonitis set in. "For four days," she says, "Tom, Sr., and I stayed at the hospital as his life hovered in the balance." The Judge remembers well the pain and the worry. Does she remember having any doubts or feelings of guilt? "No," she replies thoughtfully, "I realized that many children have reading problems, and that medical crises occur even when mother is always on home base."

Daughter Irene's reading problem stubbornly persisted through high school, even causing difficulty in language studies during her freshman year of college. Fortunately, she made top grades in math and science courses and earned a grade average that was good enough (along with fine LSAT scores) to bring her admission to the University of Virginia Law School. Graduated in 1972 and married to a fellow graduate the following year, Irene, Jr., now lives and works in New York.

Tom, Jr., was near the top of his high school class, and a captain of the debate team. At Yale, he was a member of crew and took a double major in economics and electrical engineering. After graduation, he spent five years in the Navy. At the height of the War, he was flying helicopters in Vietnam. Pointing to her now nearly white hair, the Judge says that, for her and for Tom, Sr., this year was a lifetime. On discharge, Tom, Jr., entered Vanderbilt University Law School. He's been a patent lawyer for some years.

Judge Scott recalls that when Irene, Jr., was in elementary school, she was unhappy, for a time, that her mother did not stay home like the mothers of her friends. The Judge explained that work was important to her and that it did not mean she cared any less for her children—any more than their father's working affected his feelings for his family. Over time, her daughter's concerns evaporated. Tom, Jr., doesn't remember ever thinking, as a child, that it was odd or unfortunate that his mother worked. "For one thing," he says, "it was all I had ever known since babyhood, so I just accepted it. Also, I saw women in other professions on a regular basis." For years, the Scott children were attended by a woman dentist and a woman orthodontist.

Both children were very proud of their mother as honors came her way. Both can recall the excitement surrounding her nomination for the judgeship on the U.S. Tax Court in 1959. At this time, the Judge was serving as Special Assistant to the Chief Counsel at IRS. It was a tough job. It brought work on the most troublesome cases and, also, a good bit of contact with outside lawyers. "Therefore, I wasn't surprised when two prominent members of the tax bar made an appointment to see me," she says, "but I was astonished when they told me their business." They had come to ask her if she would be willing to serve on the Tax Court. As members of the committee that would review the qualifications of nominees, they assured her of the enthusiasm among tax lawyers for her appointment as a judge.

Judge Scott's appointment cleared the Senate without difficulty, as did her reappointment in 1972 to a full fifteen-year term. Like many southerners in the capital, the Judge was acquainted with the members of Congress from her home state. As it happens, she was not related to any of them. But it would not have been unusual, for in those less-mobile days, an intricate network of family ties spread across Alabama and other southern states. Southerners who "keep up," as Judge Scott has done, can name kin in most of the counties of the state. The phenomenon amazes those who come to Washington from the big states of the North and East. Judge Scott respects tradition. She may not see them often, but she knows her cousins and the prominent Alabamans—where they live and what they are doing.

Her own home, in spite of her busy life, reflects the same respect for the durable customs of less hectic times in the South. No longer manned by a housekeeper, the Scott home in suburban Arlington is modest in size but packed with family treasures, especially pictures. A wedding picture calls forth the story about the veil of grandmother Peach Feagin, used by Irene, Sr., and remade into a cap for Irene, Jr.'s, wedding. More stories surround the 1908 photo of Arthur Feagin and the Auburn football team, the men and Coach Heisman in dark jerseys with neatly combed hair and solid, squarish faces—all staring straight into the camera.

Tales accompany the snapshots taken at the house on Chesapeake Bay where the Scotts have, for years, spent weekends. Here they swim, hike, sometimes golf, and take *other people* fishing. Fishing is one of the principal lures of the Bay, but the Judge does not enjoy it. It isn't surprising. It's hard to imagine her sitting quietly, immobilized, in a boat. Moving, nearly always talking, the Judge hurries through the days with few wasted minutes. In her home, she scurries to make the visitor comfortable. Conducting a non-stop dialogue, she prepares an impromptu meal she describes as "casual." Quick-frozen vegetables appear on French china plates, coffee from a sterling pot. Nearby cabinets in the dining room are bursting with settings of china, silver, and crystal collected by relatives in decades past.

The Judge herself brings coffee to the visitor with the morning call. "I can't wake up without coffee," she says. For four decades, Tom, Sr., has brought her a cup of coffee each morning in the bedroom. It is hard to believe that the Judge needs a spur of any sort. Her energy is so visible—even her laugh seems motorized, attached to some power source deep within. A generous conversationalist, the Judge talks on, not idly or nervously, but with a steady flow, sharing the panorama of ideas, recollections, and comments that move through her active mind.

A trained trial lawyer, the Judge is quick to move to key issues in any discussion, impatient with the trivial. Years of experience enable her to frame questions that will bare crucial facts, to expose weaknesses in any argument. Her law clerks, both top law graduates, stretch to keep up as the Judge leads discussions of cases under study. In offices adjacent to that of the Judge, the clerks, along with two secretaries, work to keep the Judge abreast of happenings related to the docket of nearly seven hundred cases that may be assigned to her in any given year.

In the stunning new building on Second Street in northwest Washington, there are office suites for each of the sixteen judges. Most of their work is done independently, but twice a month, they get together for "court review" sessions in which key cases and appeals are discussed. They meet in the huge conference room adjacent to the larger office of the Chief Judge. The new Tax Court building also houses a large law library with stacks on rollers, to allow for change and expansion. Nearby is a small room where the law clerks can be found often at the terminals of the Lexis computer into which most of the "literature of tax" has been programmed.

Two floors below is a large room filled with machinery of an entirely different kind—a treadmill and other weight-control devices. Judge Scott, who diets, often spends lunch hours here. It is consistent with her efficient life-style. "It brings a double benefit," she says. "I don't eat and I work off pounds at the same time."

Of the three courtrooms in the building, only one is large enough for the full court, because they seldom sit "en banc." Cases are most often heard by judges sitting alone, in other federal courtrooms. The smaller courtrooms in this building are used for local cases and for motions on cases that have been, or will be, tried elsewhere.

Each year, each of the judges conducts seven or eight sessions in different locations throughout the country. On each trip, some seventy or eighty cases are likely to be on the docket. The bulky files are sent from Washington in large trunks. The huge packages don't intimidate Judge Scott, who can move deftly through pounds of paper to glean the key documents. Most court sessions are scheduled for two weeks, but their length is uncertain. Several settlements sometimes bring early return to Washington. Each session, however, the Judge can be fairly certain that she will bring back from five to ten cases in which decisions must be made and opinions written. The Judge and her clerks roll up their sleeves for this task. It is the heart of the court's work.

The cases that go to decision often involve complicated facts and, usually, the knottiest points of law. Frequently, millions of dollars may be at stake. More important, says the Judge, is the consideration of the precedent set. It is the rare case that stands apart; the rare holding that does not affect a host of other taxpayers.

Major revisions of federal tax laws occur infrequently, but some changes are made at nearly every session of Congress. Dozens of lawyers at IRS keep busy drafting regulations to match the statutes. Judge Charles (Jim) Simpson, who serves with Judge Scott, spent many years doing this work before being appointed to the court. Over the years, countless rulings concerning the application of laws and regulations have burst forth from the huge IRS headquarters building on the north side of the Mall. Tax Court Judges are, in most cases, final arbiters of disputes about the meaning of these rulings, regulations, and laws. It is interpretation at the highest level. It requires precise attention to detail, a clear view of the larger issues, and, most of all, a vast knowledge of the intricacies of the United States tax laws.

Judge Scott exhibits all of these qualities, and the lawyers who practice before the court hold her in high regard. For the most part, Judge Scott's carefully drafted opinions have served as valuable guides to tax practitioners. Few of her decisions are appealed to the U.S. Circuit Courts. Only four of her cases have gone the final step to the U.S. Supreme Court; only one was reversed there.

Judge Scott can't estimate her working hours each week because her schedule is so irregular. Although she describes herself as an "accomplished skimmer," a bulky briefcase goes home with her each night. Precious hours are consumed just in keeping up with developments in the tax field; poring over "advance sheets" and other reports.

Asked about the best background preparation for law

school and for legal work, the Judge hesitates. "I studied political science because it was then the recommended pre-law major." She advises young people to study whatever interests them, but she thinks the physical sciences and math are perhaps the best preparation. "Frankly," she says, "I enjoyed political science, but I don't think it is really demanding enough. It doesn't prepare you for the kind of studying you need to do to succeed in law school or practice." Apparently, however, Irene Feagin was not unduly hampered. In three years of law school, she earned only one "C" and, at graduation, she stood second in her class. She entered law school before getting her undergraduate degree, under a "combined program" that was popular then. Today, combined programs are offered by a few law schools, but requirements for admission to them are stiff and competition is great.

Activities have been an important part of Judge Scott's life. In high school, she played basketball and was advertising manager of the yearbook. During college, the YWCA consumed much of her time, as did dramatic ventures of various kinds. She says perhaps this interest was inherited from her Aunt Lucy, a determined careerwoman who, until into her eighties, ran the Feagin School of Dramatic Art in New York City—a training base for many well-known theater personalities.

A member of the National Association of Women Lawyers, the Judge has long been a booster of better jobs for women, in government and elsewhere. She was delighted when Cynthia Hall was appointed to the Tax Court in 1972 and hopes other female colleagues will join them soon. Asked if she feels her sex has ever been a disadvantage—or an advantage —in her own career, she hedges a bit. She readily notes that it probably closed her out of practice with firms in the early days but, always fair, she adds that there were few jobs for anyone then. How about government? She thinks there was some initial reluctance, but insists that, once she got her foot inside the door of the IRS, it vanished—at least for her.

She does remember minor "incidents." When she joined the Excess Profits Tax Council, a friend told her that he had opposed her appointment because he "didn't want a woman around." Looking him in the eye, she said, "I'll forget what you said, if you'll forget that I am a woman." She reports that they got along fine after that. "I have been *lucky*," she says. "I really do not think that I was ever denied a promotion or an advance in grade level on account of being a woman." She does believe that many promotions were withheld from women lawyers in government over the years, and she says that she personally knows of instances.

How does she assess the situation today? "I think that most promotions up to Grade Fourteen proceed without regard to sex. Questions come when there are opportunities for moves to the higher grades. It is a fact," she says, "that, even today, there are very few women in any government agencies who have achieved Grades Sixteen or Seventeen." Why? Judge Scott notes that most of the jobs at these upper grade levels involve the supervision of others. She feels that even when a woman's mastery of the work is accepted, there is a question about administrative ability. She thinks that in some quarters there is still a reluctance to place a woman in a position where she has to manage a large organization.

Knowing all of these things, does the Judge encourage women to enter the legal field? Enthusiastic, she nods affirmatively. "I think the legal field offers spectacular opportunities for women. I am delighted that my daughter is a lawyer." What would she say if daughter Irene asked her advice about combining a career and a family? "Well," laughs the Judge, "she should know a lot about it from first-hand experience." Clearly, her daughter cannot help but know something about the rewards—and the price tag. Facing the challenge, she might well feel as her mother did that first day on the bench in the New York courtroom when she said, "I was awed, but not scared."

INDEX

ABOUT THE AUTHOR

Elinor Porter Swiger has written and lectured extensively about the law. Her *The Law and You: A Handbook for Young People,* a Junior Literary Guild selection (1973), and later books, *Careers in the Legal Profession* and *Law in Everyday Life* are widely used as school and family references. Married to a lawyer and the mother of three sons, Mrs. Swiger was graduated from the College of Law, Ohio State University, is a member of the Ohio Bar, and formerly served as attorney for the U.S. government in Washington, D.C.

In this book, Mrs. Swiger highlights the careers of a dozen colleagues who have been elevated to positions of highest honor and leadership. Biographees are from varying backgrounds and received their law degrees during the period from 1934 to 1964. They are outstanding lawyers and also, among them, mothers to twenty-three exemplary children. Their modes of meeting the challenge of combining careers with motherhood, their battles for legal education and legal employment, the fascinating work they do today are detailed in the book.

"I wrote the stories of these women," says Mrs. Swiger, "in part as a tribute to them, and in part to offer to the thousands of young women who are today considering legal careers, some encouraging blueprints as well as generous amounts of candid comment from twelve true experts."